Jean Toomer's 1923

TEACHING **CANE**

STUDIES IN AFRICAN AND AFRICAN-AMERICAN CULTURE

James L. Hill
General Editor

Vol. 9

PETER LANG
New York • Washington, D.C./Baltimore • Bern
Frankfurt am Main • Berlin • Brussels • Vienna • Oxford

Chezia Thompson Cager

TEACHING Jean Toomer's 1923
CANE

PETER LANG
New York • Washington, D.C./Baltimore • Bern
Frankfurt am Main • Berlin • Brussels • Vienna • Oxford

Library of Congress Cataloging-in-Publication Data

Thompson-Cager, Chezia.
Teaching Jean Toomer's 1923 Cane / Chezia B. Thompson Cager.
p. cm. — (Studies in African and African-American culture; vol. 9)
Includes bibliographical references.
1. Toomer, Jean, 1894-1967. Cane. 2. Toomer, Jean, 1894-1967—Study and teaching.
3. African Americans in literature—Study and teaching.
4. African Americans in literature. I. Title. II. Series.
PS3539.O478C338 2004   813'.52--dc22   2003027711
ISBN 0-8204-2492-7
ISSN 0890-4847

Bibliographic information published by **Die Deutsche Bibliothek.**
Die Deutsche Bibliothek lists this publication in the "Deutsche
Nationalbibliografie"; detailed bibliographic data is available
on the Internet at http://dnb.ddb.de/.

Cover artwork by Angelo Alcasabas

The paper in this book meets the guidelines for permanence and durability
of the Committee on Production Guidelines for Book Longevity
of the Council of Library Resources.

© 2006 Peter Lang Publishing, Inc., New York
29 Broadway, New York, NY 10006
www.peterlang.com

Printed in the United States of America

This book is dedicated to

▼ My grandmothers Ida and Lova (Mary Ellen), who came to talk to me to tell me not to be afraid to do *this* work, and to my grandfathers Frederick and Richard, who came later with important information;

▼ My students spanning thirty years of teaching in elementary school, high school, two-year college, public university settings, elite college settings, and finally the third-ranking art school in the nation, The Maryland Institute College of Art;

▼ Nannie, Doris, Miss Noreen, Aunt Florence, Miss Essie, Uncle Tom, Miss Pearl, Miss Carrie, and all my neighbors at 4414 Maffitt: The Lincoln Court Apartments, who protected and guided me through the minefield of my environment when I was completely defenseless;

▼ Lula Vaughn, her daughter Betsy Ward, The Girl Scouts of America, and LaBertha Blair, who taught me that style is having stamina;

▼ Dr. "Pete" Granville H. Jones and Dr. Jan Cohn, who as my sensitive and astute dissertation directors at Carnegie-Mellon University nurtured both me and this book. Your words and your wisdom are always with me;

▼ Members of my dissertation committee: Dr. Juris Seleniks and Dr. Lois Fowler;

▼ Dr. James Hill, who said yes first for Peter Lang Publishing;

▼ Madame Dorothy Thomas Matlock, Madame Carolyn May, and Madame Ella B. Silance, who—as my accelerated class English instructors—rescued me at Charles Sumner High School and gave me a vision of myself that has continually guided me;

- ▼ Dr. Kenneth Billups, who taught me to make music to heal myself;
- ▼ Professor Josiah Cox, who taught me to think creatively;
- ▼ Editor Melba Sweets and *The St. Louis American Newspaper,* who taught me to write;
- ▼ Chancellor William H. Danforth, Dean Burton Wheeler, Dr. Gloria White, and the members of the faculty and staff of Washington University (and particularly the Black Studies Program), who believed the impossible was possible and gave me immense opportunities for personal growth;
- ▼ For the members of the cast of the first and only complete production of *Cane*—for those still with us and those who have passed on—thank you for believing in the value artistic academic work can have for the whole community. Your legacy lives;
- ▼ Elizabeth McPherson and Richard Friedrick, who as Dean of Humanities and English Department Chairman at Forest Park Community College encouraged me to pursue a doctoral degree and made funds available to do the initial primary research that led to the first production of *Cane* in the Mildred E. Bastian Center for Performing Arts;
- ▼ My parents, Mr. and Mrs. James Henry Thompson, Sr., whose life work undergirds my understanding of *Cane* and the function of literature;
- ▼ Carlene Wendy Morgan, Jacki McKinney, Emelda Jones, Dorue Johnson, and Myrtle Major, who babysat me in the last months of my pregnancy and delivery to birth both my child and the initial *Cane* study;
- ▼ The child of my body and my heart, Chezia Thompson Cager, Jr., who inherits Jean Toomer's legacy as a conflicted American;
- ▼ My beloved husband, Mark Lorne Strand, who came just in time to put my life and my work in perspective and to help me recognize what I should have already known about my sight;
- ▼ Axè.

CONTENTS

List of Figures ix

PROLOGUE

Prologue: A Teacher's Simple Observations xiii
 by Dorothy Thomas Matlock
Preface xix
Acknowledgments xxiii

CONTACT

1. Thematic Overview: Using the Vertical Technique to Analyze *Cane* 1
2. A Structural Analysis of *Cane* Using the Vertical Technique 13
3. The Vertical Technique—Sociological and Historical Groundings 47

ENGAGEMENT

4. Using the Blues Motif to Analyze *Cane* 55
5. Jean Toomer: The Relationship of Biographical Material to
 Understanding *Cane* 77
6. Intersecting Lines: Early Twentieth-Century Movements
 Touching Jean Toomer and *Cane* 93

EPIPHANY

Epiphany: Toward a Unifying Theory 123

Appendix: The Poetic Essay Form: An Alternative Writing Invention 131
Notes 135
Bibliography 141

FIGURES

1.1 Traditional Plot Progression   2
1.2 Diagram of Vertical Technique   2
1.3 Four Cycles of the Vertical Technique   12
2.1 *Cane*'s Four Cycles   13
2.2 Black Time: The Reality Versus the Myth   14
2.3 Georgia: The Empire State of Lynching   27
2.4 A Lynching Map of the United States   28
2.5 The *Crisis* Anti-Lynching Ad   29
2.6 Karintha as a Child   30
2.7 The Narrator and a Fainting Fernie Mae Rose   31
2.8 Bob Stone   32
2.9 Tom Burwell   33
2.10 The Narrator and Avey   34
2.11 Bona and Paul   35
2.12 Scene from Kabnis—The Party   36
2.13 Kabnis and Carrie Kate   37
3.1 Diagram of the Vertical Technique   47
4.1 Diagram Tracing the Generation of the Blues Motif   56
4.2 Female Stereotypes in *Cane*   75
4.3 Economic Status of the Women in *Cane*   76
6.1 Archival Review of *Cane* Performance, April 1978   115
6.2 Archival Review of *Cane* Performance, April 1978   116
6.3 Archival Review of *Cane* Performance, April 1978   118
A.1 Reader Response Model   129

PROLOGUE

PROLOGUE
A Teacher's Simple Observations

The legendary twenty-two-year head of the English Department at Charles Sumner High School, Dorothy Thomas Matlock, single-handedly introduced *Cane* to the St. Louis Public School system in 1965. This poetic essay describes her three major encounters with *Cane,* marking historical moments in the regional development of African-American cultural consciousness.

PROLOGUE

Cane is a kaleidoscope of many issues, but one of the most important issues that it presents is the necessity of preserving African-American culture's authentic art forms. As a single work, *Cane* presents the power and beauty of the African-American image in a way that is literally unforgettable, and thus achieves the goal of preservation. There was nothing in my elementary, high school, or college curriculum that presented African-American literature as a critical part of American literature. Phillis Wheatley, Paul Laurence Dunbar, and Langston Hughes were likely the only writers mentioned in anthologies or introduced in class. One certainly could not major or minor in a subject area that would explore African-American literature or history until the 1970s, even at historically African-American colleges and universities.

Nevertheless, my tenure as head of the English Department at Charles Sumner High School (the oldest African-American high school west of the Mississippi River in St. Louis, Missouri) led me to believe that something else was needed in the development of African-American culture in high school. My suspicion was confirmed by what has come to be known as the Black Is Beautiful Movement in the 1960s. The greater part of the

African-American community yelled in unison with James Brown, "Say It Loud: I'm Black and I'm Proud!" The song spurred the vernacular culture, which then forced the elite culture to challenge its own ideas of what was right, what was beautiful, what was empowering for the great mass of African-American people in St. Louis. But you could see this movement coming in the change of hairstyles and people wearing bright colors and African stripes. I could see it coming and, as department chair, I felt that it was my responsibility to develop a strategy to make this new cultural movement work in the best interest of our students. I started my own research.

CONTACT

Close Encounter of the First Kind

My research led me to the unknown, unsung slave narratives, the prolific nineteenth-century African-American writers, and the Harlem Renaissance. The Harlem Renaissance looked every bit like what was then happening before my eyes: cultural déjà vu. The ethnic orientation, the elevation of African persona, the link to a transcontinental diaspora family, and the innovation in language (as an attempt to redefine our reality in ways that would stop the denigration of our essential selves) were all hallmarks of the Harlem Renaissance. I discovered that the book that did all of these things the best, without proselytizing the reader, was *Cane* by a man named Jean Toomer. I was hypnotized, mesmerized, and in love with the book and the author. I taught it for the first time in 1965 to the freshman accelerated English class, which included an impoverished but aspiring Chezia Thompson. Though other African-American writers were included in the revised curriculum, I don't think *Cane* was generally included in the 1960s or 1970s. I didn't personally teach *Cane* again until thirteen years later. However, this 1965 freshman class went on to do some of the first interdisciplinary work conscientiously linking African-American culture across the curriculum. A sample of the activities executed included: performances of the South African musical drama *Lost in the Stars,* orchestral cantatas including "They Call Her Moses," "Song of America," and the Congolese "Missa Luba Mass" in Kenneth Billups's choir class; a study of the Dunham (dance) technique in gym class with Pelaja Green; cooperative ventures with the school band performing symphonic works by African-American composers; and replicating Booker T. Washington's experiments in Josiah Cox's biology class. Early in the 1970s I recommended two English courses be introduced into the English curriculum in the St. Louis Public Schools—Black Writers and Afro-American Writers. They were introduced, accepted, and institutionalized, forming a collective strategy for preserving African-American literature. A course called Black Humanities was also accepted. It consisted of the art, literature, and music from ancient Africa to the present time, and the late Chester Bowie and I team-taught this course for more than twenty years.

Close Encounter of the Second Kind

In 1978 Chezia Thompson sent me an invitation to bring my class to the first production of the complete text of *Cane* at the Mildred E. Bastian Center for the Performing Arts. Using her previous study with me and poet K. Curtis Lyle (at Washington University), she created a script linking all of the parts of *Cane*. Moved by the unique opportunity to engage the text again, I arranged for nine busloads of students from nine different high schools to go to a special matinee performance. The teams of teachers bringing the students had discussed the book with me, and all of the students had been provided with photocopies of section one of *Cane* to read before attending the performance. (None of the schools had these texts available.) The performance was a collaboration between Chezia's English class community college students and the community of non-equity actors. My high school students were completely amazed that literature could be so visceral, so expressive, so emotional, so ideologically challenging, so mystifyingly uncategorizable and be so much like people that they knew. The students came back to school and found *Cane* in libraries all over St. Louis or ordered it at book stores. Without any further assignment from their teachers, many of them read the whole book and met with other students from other high schools in study groups to talk about what it "really" meant and to share their experiences in relationship to the text. I was invited as "the expert reader" to many of these sessions. This first class of Toomerites would go on to colleges and jobs with the ideology of cultural affirmation, and in the 1980s they would ground the earlier founding of African-American Studies departments and Black Literary curricula's initiatives at every imaginable level. I saw it as literature acting as the force it was invented to be in the development of the human mind. Keeping alive the tradition ... preserving our cultural heritage.

Close Encounter of the Third Kind

My third encounter with *Cane* occurred when one of the students from the second encounter institutionalized *Cane* even further in the public school system. In 1993, Dr. Lynn Beckwith, the founder and first president of the Metropolitan St. Louis Alliance of Black School Educators, invited me to be the presenter and consultant for the Division of State and Federal Programs—Harlem Renaissance in-service sessions. I worked primarily with Title I teachers, under the auspices of the St. Louis public schools.

ENGAGEMENT

Poet Laureate of Detroit and Lotus Press founder Naomi Madgett Long gave me the phone number of the now-dreadlocked Carnegie-Mellon University graduate, poet, and Professor of Language and Literature at Maryland Institute College of Art, Dr. Chezia Thompson Cager Strand. When I called her recently to discuss her analysis of *Cane,* in preparation for talking to my local reading club about it, I was surprised and delighted to discover that she remembered me as well as I remembered her and that our link was Jean Toomer's *Cane.* She came to St. Louis to assist me on April 19, 2003, at the Saturday Friends Reading Group meeting at the Julia Davis Branch Library. Librarians and members of other reading groups attended. Our discussion almost forty years later after we first met was delightful, scintillating, intellectual, and strangely weird. It was disjunctive between literary cosmologies and theories of lunar phase transitions, theories of feminist literature and "black aesthetics," the politics of historicism and Toomer's unique position as a non-Negro in African-American literature. We chanted Karintha's insignia lines together, "our skin is like dust." The three meetings of the literary club to discuss *Cane* were equally intriguing and mind-altering. I, having retired from teaching long ago, wondered again at the power of this book in my life and in the lives of others. This book had forged a seamless friendship between me and four generations of students, who still visit me and talk about that moment of clarity, when the culture to which they were connected became a shining, nurturing thing, beckoning them to challenge irrational and racist mythologies. It beckoned them to push toward the goal of the high calling of excellence as an example of how African-Americans could reinvent themselves in the American mainstream, which had intentionally misrepresented their real historic selves.

Jean Toomer's genius was an overpowering experience for me. The sheer beauty of his figurative language is still captivating. The variety of characterizations provides an exotic menu of physical and emotional types of Americans inhabiting the landscape of 1923. The description of the landscape as various people and the description of the people as part of nature resonated in my soul. There was something organic, synchronous, melodious even in the way Toomer portrayed things in *Cane*. He saw firsthand the brutality, the hardships, and the social and economic oppression of blacks in the South; but he also saw the dignity and strength of the black folk culture. *Cane* tracks African-Americans' great migration north, where they had to compete with a more virulent form of Jim Crow and the beginning of the machine's takeover of American workers' jobs and lives. *Cane* depicts language as both a tool and a weapon within the American landscape. *Cane* reconstructs biblical truths and explodes them as ontology-specific snapshots from one kind of camera. Anything you read or write you bring yourself (and in this case your Lord as well) to it.

Cane used an unconventional structure to teach an unconventional lesson in 1923 that is still relevant today. The structure makes sense without conforming to any known literary genre. It is more like the structure of thought. (Talk to Chezia about Noam Chomsky and Paulo Freire.) That's why despite elusive reviews, it continues to be read: More than read, it is celebrated! I believe that once in a lifetime a truth is uncovered to push mankind into a new state of being. *Cane* is that truth in twentieth-century America.

One of *Cane*'s most successful devices lies in the way Toomer depicts southern women as dusky goddesses, living humble, embattled lives in the red clay of Georgia—the red clay that resonates the first streak of red in the sunrise and the last streak of red in the sunset. Toomer's *Cane* women are covered with dust and legacy. They are all pregnant with the expectancy that the light of illumination will shine through the dust and set their dusky auras ablaze, singing in cane fields.

EPIPHANY

I am in my golden years, but *Cane* still makes me feel and know that I am a beautiful black woman. What I have tried to do is paint Toomer as someone who appreciated African-American culture and the physical beauty of black women. The dignity of the black folk culture is what he was emphasizing. *Cane* suggests that there is an intrinsic strength in African-American culture. While there may be more books attempting to do that today, they rarely approach *Cane*'s integral artistry. *Cane* helped me to discover my inner beauty and my self-pride in a very powerful way, in an age when African-American women were taught to imitate white culture and physiognomy. *Cane* still speaks to me, resounding in my soul in "dream-fluted" waves.

Dorothy Thomas Matlock

PREFACE

A brave new century has engaged an age-old concept defining American literature by the writer's skin color. Technological and scientific discoveries in the late twentieth and twenty-first centuries have caused us to question many areas of knowledge once considered indisputable. Our quest has become a cultural obsession to understand such questions as: (1) How does DNA define what a human being is at the cellular level? (2) How can the personal be differentiated from the private in e-mail or other telecommunications? (3) What exactly is "race" in an America that still includes such a designation on census forms and other official documents? What these three questions have in common is their intrinsic link to modern American culture and the proposition that puts the humanities at the center of defining how cultures progress. Eugene Pinchback Toomer (who changed his name to Nathan Jean Toomer or Jean Toomer) posed such questions at a time before the technology was available to even consider these possibilities, much less question and explore them.

Jean Toomer's life and work form a unique bridge between the writing of nineteenth- and twentieth-century American writers, including Charles Chesnutt and Paul Laurence Dunbar. Toomer's life remains a model of the American melting pot theory during and after the Atlantic Slave Trade. Almost a century later, his major work is still an enigma that invites dissection in order to make conventional literary sense. In this technological age, extracts from his work still provoke the same questions: (1) What is a human being at the cellular level? (2) At what point are the personal self and personal property considered a public self and public property? and finally (3) Is racial difference a reality or a myth? As with many writers of African-American descent past and present, his work is analyzed more in relation to the color of his skin than by its own merit. In Toomer's case, it was an inconvenient and awkward fit for which necessity found a historical rationale.

Houston A. Baker, Jr., in *The Journey Back: Issues in Black Literature and Criticism* (page xii), says, "There has been a great deal of muddled thinking about black literature during the recent past" by American literary scholars in general. The tendency to compare its structural analysis to a particular European-American writer and its contextual analysis to defining the experience of racial difference in America negates the assignation of the creative impulse to invent something that did not exist before. It negates the impulse to celebrate—not apologize, defend, or proselytize—the self-affirming act of writing. It negates the concepts of ontology and epistemology as organic person-specific attributes and assigns the writer a group identity before considering the writer's creative vision in the work.

This book presents a different way of looking at Jean Toomer's *Cane* and explores strategies to use with a view to teach its vital lessons in a more holistic way. It situates *Cane* historically within American culture and utilizes Toomer's training as an artist and philosopher to describe an analytical structure that incorporates Toomer's Euro-American and African-American viewpoints. It also utilizes his physical education training, including dance, and his associations with African-American visual artists such as Rex Gorleigh, that broadened his base of knowledge from which to create his literary work. The analytical structure needed to decipher *Cane* must have a concept of culture at its core definition of linguistic discourse. That discourse must allow for peculiarities in both cultural priority and historical pattern without segmenting the American literary historical consciousness within the work in an artificial way.

The two challenges of this book are: (1) to make sense of *Cane* without reducing its multiplicity of complex conceptual images, superimposed upon what appears to be an irregular and strange literary structure; and (2) to define a language of instruction that can reveal the text in its entirety to generations of readers as a coherent and memorable work. Some of the previous research on both Toomer and *Cane* was utilized to accomplish this task. Nevertheless, this study is meant to be neither a biographical review of Toomer's life nor a critique of the analytical work previously published. Moreover, this text explores a more culturally grounded view of literary analysis to invent a structure that is particularly relevant to teaching *Cane* but is also applicable to other work throughout the African diaspora. It is a structure that requires the viewpoint of an artist versed in the performing arts, trained in literary analysis, and actively participating in the act of creative writing. Like many of his Harlem Renaissance/Lost Generation literary compatriots, Toomer was all this and more—a writer able to converse with multiple traditions in the ecstatic voice of a great bard.

Chezia Thompson Cager

ACKNOWLEDGMENTS

I would like to thank and acknowledge the time and talent of the following people and organizations who helped make this publication possible:

▼ Vincent Fitzpatrick, Curator and Librarian, The Mencken Archives at Enoch Pratt Library—Baltimore, for making the wealth of the Mencken Archives available;

▼ Simmona Simmons-Hodo, The Albin O. Kuhn Library—University of Maryland Baltimore County, for assistance with the selected bibliography;

▼ Brian Gordon, photographer, for the 1978 *Cane* production photographs;

▼ Chris King for permission to reprint from the *St. Louis American* archives;

▼ Gladys Coggswell for permission to reprint archival articles;

▼ Kathy Dunlop, Dean of Communication Division, St. Louis Community College at Forest Park for permission to reprint archival articles from *The Scene*;

▼ Oberlin College Press for permission to reprint William Kulik's translation of Max Jacob's "Moon Poem" in *The Selected Poems of Max Jacob*.

▼ Excerpts from Langston Hughes' "The Negro and the Racial Mountain." Reprinted with permission from the June 23, 1926, issue of *The Nation* magazine. For subscription information, call 1-800-333-8586. Portions of each week's *Nation* magazine can be accessed at http://www.thenation.com.

▼ Graphic illustration and "Black Time:The Reality Versus the Myth" is reprinted with permission from author, Bonnie Barthold from *Black Time: Fiction in Africa, the Caribbean, and the United*

States published by Yale University Press, who is the sole copyright hodler.

▼ Howard University Press for permission to reprint excerpts from *The Wayward and the Seeking;*

▼ The citations from author Jean Toomer's *Cane* are reprinted with permission of LIVERIGHT Publishing Corporation (as a subsidiary company of W.W. Norton and Company) who is the sole copyright holder;

▼ Crisis Publishing Co., Inc., the publisher of the magazine of the National Association for the Advancement of Colored People, for the use of the graphics and citations on lynching in the 1920s and the Great Migration.

CONTACT

CHAPTER 1
Thematic Overview: Using the Vertical Technique to Analyze Cane

The Vertical Technique sets experiences in *Cane* into four archetypal stages to reflect the history of Africana people in the New World. These stages appear to reflect a developing linear plot (See Figure 1.1) that seems typical in the Western literary tradition. However, using this formula to analyze *Cane* only frustrates the reader. The characters appear to change every few pages. There are major shifts in the setting. The conflicts seem more dependent on inaction than action. There does not appear to be a climax or a resolution of plot or character as the reader traditionally thinks of them. However, using Cyclical Phenomenal Time and a knowledge of the history of African-Americans (to help clarify *Cane*'s nontraditional portrayal of African-Americans in the New World), the reader can decipher the four stages of the Vertical Technique as shown in Figure 1.2 on page 2.

These four stages describe the European incursion into Africana history as a geographic literary movement similar to the lives of men and women in the South and the North in America. Although the stages occur consecutively, they overlap at points and help to organize *Cane*'s plot through the development of the omniscient narrator—at first a nameless observer, then a nameless person in the active voice, then a person with a name passing as a Euro-American, and finally, a named person in the same pastoral setting that appears at the beginning of the poetic drama. The interlocking characterizations show the development of the mulatto male narrator's vision of American life at the start of the twentieth century. From the very beginning of *Cane,* the reader encounters the first component of the Vertical Technique as an attack on a child in a pastoral setting.

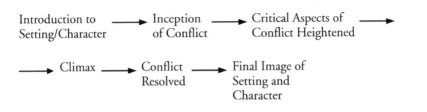

▶ **Figure 1.1 Traditional Plot Progression**

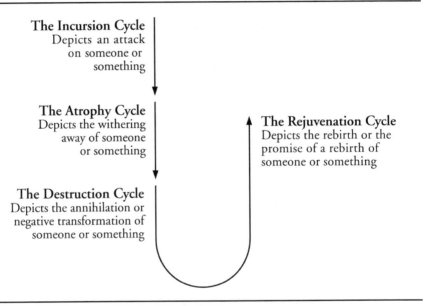

▶ **Figure 1.2 Diagram of Vertical Technique**

THE INCURSION CYCLE

The Attack on the Reality of Southern Rural Life in the African-American Community

Place: The South, the Countryside in Georgia, 1923

Karintha's characterization represents the result of the abuse of African-American feminine beauty and sexuality in the South, where (because of her use as a reproductive animal during the Atlantic Slave Trade) her body has always been taken for granted, or been available in exchange for money, goods, services, or protection.

> Her skin is like dusk,
> O can't you see it
> Her skin is like dusk,
> When the sun goes down ...
> Karintha is a woman. Men do not know that
> the soul of her was a growing thing ripened
> too soon. They will bring their money; they will
> die not having found it out.[1]

In the second portrait, Becky's characterization represents the consequences of breaking established social/sexual taboos in the rural South. The heretic Euro-American woman provides a different model of behavior that southern culture cannot condone and which directly accuses Euro-American men of being either inadequate or morally wrong in their racial attitudes.

> Becky was the white woman who
> had two Negro sons. She's dead; they've
> gone away ...
> Who gave it to her ... She wouldn't tell.[2]

Carma's characterization represents the consequences that a woman incurs when she actualizes her personal and sexual freedom. The physically strong African-American woman who insists upon "taking lovers" of her own choice provides another model of behavior that southern culture could not condone and indirectly accuses African-American men of being either weak, dishonest, or inferior to her.

> Carma in overalls, and strong as any
> man ... She does not sing; her body
> is a song ... Her husband's in the
> gang. And it's her fault he got
> there. Working with a contractor,
> he was away most of the time. She
> had others. No one blames her for
> that ...[3]

So the Incursion Cycle has identified an attack on the African-American family at the level of child and mother, and husband and wife, which significantly undermines the integrity of the structures that had held those relationships together. As those relationships deteriorate, the culture itself begins to atrophy.

THE ATROPHY CYCLE

The Continued Withering Away of Southern Rural Culture and Personality in the African-American Community

Place: Still the South, the Countryside in Georgia in 1923

The narrator bears witness to the atrophy process's effect in "Song of the Son."

> Now just before an epoch's sun declines
> Thy son, in time I have returned to thee ...

The narrator mourns the passing beauty of a twilight culture singing its own swan song in "Georgia Dusk."

> A feast of moon and men and barking hounds
> An orgy for some genius of the South
> With blood-hot eyes and cane-lipped scented
> mouth,
> Surprised in making folk-songs from soul sounds ...

Fern's character represents the problem of a woman evolving as a spiritual being in the southern social and sexual milieu. Fern is isolated/protected from the consequences of sexual appeal that Karintha, Becky, and Carma endure. She is said to "hold God" and God's bride must not be violated for fear of retribution from God. Perhaps she hoards some power or some truth that unleashed would transform the environment. Nevertheless, she appears unable to do anything with the power. She is trapped in her physical and "spiritual" spaces, watching the ineffectiveness—the atrophy of people and processes around her.

> Fern's eyes desired nothing that you
> could give her ... Men saw her eyes
> and fooled themselves. Fern's eyes
> said to them that she was easy ...
> From the train window I saw her as
> she crossed her road ... Saw her face
> flow into them, the countryside and
> something that I call God, flowing
> into them ...

"Nullo" and "Evening Song" reflect images of arrested activity in nature and in man. The falling pine needles at sunset merge with "dry moulds of cow-hoofs" unnoticed by the rabbits who travel the forest floor. In "Evening Song" "Cloine tires ... Cloine sleeps ... and Cloine dreams" in a nullo status that leaves her "curled like the sleepy waters where the moon waves start," in a mystical trance—like Fern, doing nothing as she marks time.

Place: Still the South but Moved to a Small Town's Main Street in Georgia in 1923

Esther's characterization represents the result of social isolation by caste and color and the result of the repression of that alleged abundant sexual nature that Karintha, Becky, and Carma demonstrate (as supposedly typical African-American women in the South). As the daughter of the richest colored man in town, Esther is unable to face the reality of the culture in which she lives on the periphery, watching her heart's desire—Barlo— ignore her existence. Like Cloine, she takes to the inactivity—the atrophy of dreaming. Finally, her dreams destroy reality, and then she is faced with Barlo's rejection and her own mental illness as "there is no air, no street, and the town has completely disappeared."

> Nine.
> Esther looks like a little white
> child, starched, frilled, as she
> walks slowly from her home towards
> her father's grocery store ...
> Sixteen.
> Esther begins to dream ...
> Twenty-two.
> ... Her hair thins. It looks like
> the dull silk on puny corn ears.
> Her face pales until it is the color
> of the gray dust that dances with
> dead cotton leaves ...
> Esther is twenty-seven.
> Dead dreams and a forgotten resolution
> are carried upward by the flames. They
> shan't have him. Oh they shall not. Not
> if it kills me they shan't have him ...
> ... Jeers and hoots pelter bluntly upon her back.
> She steps out. There is no air, no street, and the
> town has completely disappeared.[4]

Dreaming is one kind of altered state of reality that in other modern theories represents the act of doing. References to dreaming here signify the physical act of the body moving from awake and active in a concrete reality, to be sleeping and lying immobile in an unconscious state.

THE DESTRUCTION CYCLE

The Destruction of Rural African-American Southern Inhabitants and the Annihilation of the Illusion of Civilized Behavior in the Pastoral South

Place: Still the South and Still on a Small Town's Main Street in Georgia in 1923

"Conversion" retells the story of Esther's fall as a preoccupation with a western concept of religion. (Barlo is a preacher.) That religion, too, as Barlo reveals, is one of the tools of the atrophy process.

> Yielding to new words and a
> Weak palabra
> Of a white-faced sardonic god ... [5]

Caste by color segregation is another tool that we see in "Portrait in Georgia"; and it is a lethal weapon against a group of people facing the fire of Jim Crow laws.

> And her slim body, white as the ash
> Of black flesh after flame.[6]

"Blood-Burning Moon," the story of Louisa, portrays the result of breaking class and caste taboos in social and sexual relationships in the South. The example of an African-American female domestic worker openly sharing her affections with her Euro-American employer's son and her African-American sweetheart cannot be tolerated. If she has been chosen by the two, only one can be master and keep his dignity as a man.

> Louisa sang as she came over the crest of the hill from the white folks' kitchen. Her skin was the color of oak leaves on young trees in fall. Bob Stone, younger son of the people she worked for, loved her ... Tom Burwell, whom the whole town called Big Boy, also loved her ...

> > Red Nigger moon. Sinner!
> > Blood-Burning moon. Sinner!
> > Come out that factory door ...

> Blue flash, a steel blade slashed across Bob Stone's throat. He had a sweetish sick feeling, Blood began to flow ...

> Now Tom could be seen within the flames. Only his head, erect, lean like a blackened stone. Stench of burning flesh soaked the air. Tom's eyes popped ... She'd sing ... Perhaps Tom Burwell would come.[7]

Place: The North, Seventh Street, Washington, D.C., 1923

Toomer establishes the immense differences in environment by describing Washington, D.C., from the view on "Seventh Street." He uses "Rhobert" to alert the reader that within this less-than-natural environment, something is very wrong.

As the first woman in the northern Urban Cycle in *Cane*, Avey is a conglomeration of the attributes of the women in the Incursion and Atrophy Cycles. She reflects the modifications that occurred in the evolution of African-American womanhood moving from the country to the city at the beginning of the century. Avey is alluring; she attracts men effortlessly, like Karintha. She openly breaks the established societal and sexual code of remaining a virgin until marriage, like Becky, and exhibits an unusual maternal attitude toward the nameless narrator. She is resilient and insists on actualizing her personal and sexual freedom of choice, like Carma. As with Fern, men fool themselves about Avey and she is, indeed, victimized by their antiquated, sexist, moral standards. While she does not suffer from Esther's sexual repression, she does not appear to have or to want a meaningful love relationship. She is orphaned, isolated emotionally. Since she does not fulfill her potential as a middle-class professional woman, she is isolated socially as well. Like Louisa, Avey works doing something to financially support herself. She breaks the taboos of class that she has entered through work by refusing the privilege of being assimilated into society as a teacher—which, in the case of women, required celibacy. Unlike Louisa, who has two lovers, Avey has many lovers and admirers including the nameless narrator. Yet, for all the men, she is inextricably alone, indifferent, unaffected. Singularly, Avey's characterization represents the abused potential of intelligent, dissipated feminine power in the twentieth century. In the twenty-first century, the model of her behavior will portend a new kind of "detachment" and control to be envied.

> I gave her one burning kiss. Then she laid me in her lap as if I was a child. Helpless ... She wouldn't let me go ... Orphan Woman ... [8]

"Beehive" and "Storm Ending" are decadent images of trapped inertia. The beauty is mesmerizing in both cases. Intoxicated drone bees and thunder blossom clouds under attack by the sun are both powerless to resist their predestination.

> "Beehive"
> Within this black hive tonight there swarm a million bees; ...
> and I, a drone ...
> Getting drunk with silver honey,

Wish that I might fly out past the moon
And curl forever in some far-off farmyard flower.[9]

"Storm Ending"
Thunder blossoms gorgeously above our heads, ...
Bitten by the sun
Bleeding rain ...
And the sweet earth flying from the thunder.[10]

Dorris's characterization represents the frustration of woman as artist in society in the early twentieth century. Like Avey, men view her as a sexual object, but she is also ostracized by being classed as a "showgirl," who is different from "regular" women. Her frustration on a personal level stems from John, the object of her desire, who is overtly sterile and unable to act on his own thoughts.

Life of nigger alleys, of poolrooms and restaurants and near-beer saloons soaks into the walls of Howard Theatre ...

Soon the audiences will paint your dusk faces white and call you beautiful. (O Dance!)

O will you love me? And give me kids, and a home, and everything? ... You will if I make you. Just watch me.—

Dorris dances. She forgets her tricks. She dances ... [11]

"Her Lips Are Copper Wire" questions the interface between man as machine with the machines in his environment, upon which he is dependent—particularly in an urban environment. The juxtaposition of the two pieces of writing contrasts the function and impact of art (as dance) and technology (as a construction essential to life for communication or protection). The prose poem "Calling Jesus" anticipates the characterization of Muriel in "Box Seat."

"Calling Jesus"

Her soul is like a little thrust-tailed dog that follows her, whimpering ...

At night, when she comes home, the little dog is left in the vestibule, nosing the crack beneath the big storm door, filled with chills till morning. Someone ... will steal in ... carry it to her where she sleeps: cradled in dream-fluted cane.[12]

In the Destruction Cycle, Muriel represents the isolation of a pretentious, middle-class professional woman who has forgotten her southern, agrarian, African-American roots. As the object of Dan Moore's desires, she is constantly reminded that there are other ways to live and other values that could possibly improve the quality of her life considerably.

> Muriel comes in, shakes hands and then clicks into a high-armed seat under the orange glow of a floor-lamp. Her face is fleshy. It would tend to coarseness but for the fresh, fragrant something which is the life of it ...

> Dan looks at her, directly. Her animalism, still unconquered by zoo-restrictions and keeper taboos, stirs him ...

> Happy, Muriel? No, not happy. Your aim is wrong. There is no such thing as happiness. Life bends joy and pain, beauty and ugliness, in such a way that no one may isolate them.[13]

"Prayer" predicts the advent of Bona as a superficial person. That is, as a Euro-American (within a cultural milieu that separates the body and mind as a form of intellectualism in 1923) Bona's whiteness isn't primarily about her skin color. It is more about her problem seeing and connecting her body (as emotion) and her soul (as her higher intelligence). As "Prayer" describes her in the Destruction Cycle, she is yet one more incomplete, unhappy person.

> "Prayer"
> My body is opaque to the soul ...
> But my mind, too, is opaque to the soul.
> A closed lid is my soul's flesh-eye ...
> So weak that I have confused the body with the soul, ... [14]

In "Harvest Song" the third-person omniscient narrator who became a first-person omniscient narrator who became an active first-person narrator will become in "Bona and Paul" a first-person narrator with a name, as he engages his ongoing process of development throughout *Cane* in "Harvest Song." He is harvesting himself, his culture, and what he understands—as he uses the process of *Cane* to become self-aware. The harvesting process with grain necessitates separating it from its life-giving root and stalk—where it will eventually die and be converted to another form for consumption. The narrator's id and ego are simultaneously dying in preparation for conversion to another self-actualized form; which is the nature of the Reaper Tarot Card, as an omen of change to come.

> "Harvest Song"
> I am a reaper whose muscles set at sundown, ...
> I am a blind man who stares across the hills ...
> (Dusk is a strange fear'd sheath their blades are dull'd in.) ...
> I hunger ...
> I am a reaper ...
> My throat is dry ...

My pain is sweet.[15]

Place: Chicago, Illinois: A Segregated College Campus

In the last portrait in the Destruction Cycle (the northern section) of *Cane*, Bona's characterization reflects the hazards of breaking societal and sexual taboos in America. As a southern Euro-American woman, her upbringing has rationalized sexism (in the courtship process) and racism (in interracial relationships). Thus, she reflects the frustration of a Euro-American woman as the initiator of intimate social relationships with black men. Paul, an African-American man passing as a Euro-American man, mirrors Bona's psychosis as he struggles through his own identity crisis. All of the problems that they both sought to escape in the South are still present in Chicago. The illusion of the North, as way of life with different operative values than the South, is destroyed.

> That something beautiful is going to happen ...
> That I am going out and know her whom I brought here with
> me to the Gardens which are purple like a bed of roses would
> be at dusk.
> Paul and the black [door] man shook hands.
> When he reached the spot where they [he and Bona]
> had been standing, Bona was gone.[16]

THE REJUVENATION CYCLE

The Rebirth of Something or Someone or the Promise of Rebirth of Something or Someone

Place: The South, Small Town in Georgia, 1923

The focus of the Rejuvenation Cycle is the process that the narrator, Ralph Kabnis, goes through as he faces his cumulative psychosis about race and sex. The women who aid him are Stella and Cora, who reflect the tragedy of woman as sexual object, and Carrie Kate, who endows the Rejuvenation Cycle with its force by portraying the courage of woman as healer. The rising sun is the metaphorical symbol of the Rejuvenation Cycle.

> Stella: Usall is brought up t hate sin worse than death—
>
> Kabnis: An then before you have y eyes half open, youre made t love it if y want t live.
>
> Stella: Us never—
>
> Kabnis: Oh, I know your story: that old prim bastard over yonder and then old Calvert's office—

Stella: It wasn't them—

Kabnis: I know. They put y out of church, an then I guess th preacher came around an asked f some. But that's your body. Now me—...

Lewis: ... Can't hold them, can you? Master; slave. Soil; and the over-arching heavens. Dusk; dawn. They fight and bastardize you... .

Carrie K.: Brother Ralph is that your best Amen?

She turns him to her and take[s] his hot cheeks in her firm cool hands. Her palms drew the fever out. With its passing, Kabnis crumbles ...

... Her lips murmur, "Jesus, come."

Outside, the sun arises from its cradle ...

Gold-glowing child, it steps into the sky and sends a birth-song slanting down gray dust streets and sleepy windows of the southern town.[17]

Through the Vertical Technique as an analytical tool, it is possible to see the primary character portrayals as critical elements in the plotline and the unity of the thematic structure that chronicles the atrophy of the human psyche under specific conditions. The Vertical Technique incorporates the attempts of both the Harlem Renaissance and the Negritude Movements to communicate a kind of noncommunicable pain and a subterranean anger evolving out of African-Americans' efforts to struggle in a meaningful, dignified, and spiritually uplifting manner. The new literature, in Alain Locke's words, depicts the emergence of a "New Negro" or the twentieth-century, Western-cultivated African-American who would neither deny his culture nor abandon the country that he has helped to become rich and powerful. This chapter has introduced the reader to the Vertical Technique's basic thematic delineation of *Cane*. The next chapter uses the Vertical Technique's basic thematic structure (See Figure 1.3) to do an in-depth structural analysis of *Cane*.

Differences in the way language is used and understood, in relationship to skin color, in the American historical context.

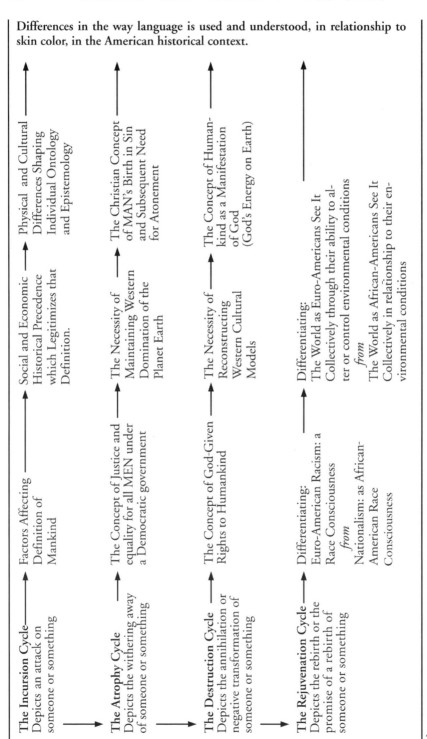

▲ Figure 1.3 Four Cycles of the Vertical Technique

CHAPTER 2
A Structural Analysis of Cane Using the Vertical Technique

I. Incursion Cycle: Karintha Reapers November Cotton Flower Becky Face Carma Song of the Son Georgia Dusk Fern Nullo Evening Song	III. Destruction Cycle: Blood Burning Moon Seventh Street Rhobert Avey Beehive Storm Ending Theater Her Lips Are Copper Wire Calling Jesus Box Seat Prayer Harvest Song Bona & Paul
II. Atrophy Cycle: Esther Conversion Portrait in Georgia	IV. Rejuvenation Cycle: Kabnis

▶ Figure 2.1 *Cane*'s Four Cycles

The Vertical Technique borrows two concepts from African culture by way of the Negritude Movement. The first concept insists on seeing Africans (African-Americans, Afro-Caribbeans) as "whole men"[1] who come from comprehensible cultures with complex linguistic forms and a repertoire of gestures that accompany those forms. The second concept argues the existence of a way of telling and feeling time differently from the Western European way. One is reminded in countless colonial and

The Linear New World and the Balancing Act

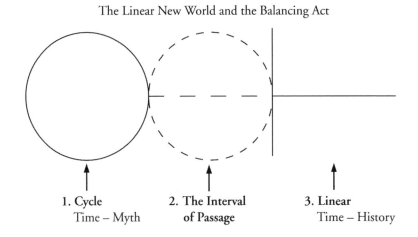

1. Cycle   2. The Interval   3. Linear
Time – Myth   of Passage   Time – History

▶ **Figure 2.2 Black Time: The Reality Versus the Myth.**
Source: Bonnie Barthold, *Black Time: Fiction of Africa, the Caribbean and the United States.* Yale University Press (New Haven and London: 1981) p. 18. "Black people have experienced time differently from white people, ... because they hav been simultaneously deprived of time and fixed in it by the color of their skin." (p. 16)

slave films that African-American people allegedly do not know the meaning of time. K. Curtis Lyle[2] calls this kind of time Phenomenal Time and, like Bonnie Barthold in *Black Time: Fiction of Africa, the Caribbean and the United States,* juxtaposes it against the European concept of Linear Time (See Figure 2.2). This study calls it Cyclic Phenomenal Time.

> The first stage represents the configuration of time in a traditional, agrarian culture—for example, pre-European Africa and ... specifically the culture of the Guinea Coast. The third stage represents the linearity time has assumed in a highly industrialized culture like that of the United States. In between is the interval of passage, the simultaneous erosion of the cycle and the development of linearity. The shift described by Wright corresponds with a movement from synchrony to diachrony in time, from a conceptualization of time that rejects change to one that is able to embrace change and, potentially at least, to lend it order. In fact, however, the diagram as given belies the potential complexity of a historic conceptualization of time, which includes "the interplay of a number of durations ... a recognition of the 'multiplicity of time.'" Instead of the unity of the cycle—a unity dependent upon the rejection of change—in Guillen's view what one has is a linear simultaneity, a diversity of linear "currents" that, taken together, characterize time during a given moment or period. In this view, diachrony assumes a far greater complexity than the diagram indicates.[3]

The Vertical Technique argues that the temporal and the nontemporal are bridgeable in the African worldview: that the conceptualization of time in *Cane* is shaped by a history and a way of life that, in turn, are shaped by one's caste and color. Barthold uses J. S. Mbiti's *African*

Religions and Philosophy, Mircea Eliade's *The Myth of the Eternal Return or, Cosmos and History,* and Willie E. Abraham's *The Mind of Africa* (1962) to reinforce the philosophical base for what she calls Cyclic Time and what this study identifies as Cyclic Phenomenal Time.

> Willie Abraham points out that the "temporal and the non-temporal" were not "unbridgeable" in the African world view, and suggests that this continuity comes out of a cyclic conceptualization of time. Janheinz Jahn remarks that "Africa is only now emerging from the age of myth ... into the mainstream of history." J. S. Mbiti asserts that "the linear concept of time, with an indefinite past, present and infinite future is practically foreign to African thinking." And according to Mircea Eliade, the culture of traditional tribal groups of this area was characterized by religious beliefs that included the cyclic regeneration of time and the abolition of history.[4]

The Vertical Technique takes this concept of Cyclic Time and divides it into four stages that approximate the stages of colonization but also replicate the process of dispossession that the black characters in Toomer's world complete. The characters in *Cane* are deprived of time as well as financial resources. The time frames of the poetic-drama show the deterioration of the African personality functioning in the linear time of the United States. Sacred time is divorced from human time, except when one enters the cane field. The first-person omniscient narrator in *Cane*'s "Fern" tells us, "Time and space have not meaning in the Cane field. No more than the interminable stalks." The manipulations of time channel the Africana personality in ways that suit the purpose of the possessors of time. Barthold chronicles this purpose as part of the legacy of the holocaust of the Atlantic Slave Trade to revise Africana history as a void where time began at the moment Africa was invaded by Europe. The revision was a necessary strategy to develop a rationale for denying Africans anywhere on Earth access to progress, as defined by Western constructs.

> In the twentieth century, being black may very well imply dwelling in a perpetually contingent state of time. Because of the relative strength of this possibility for black people, the dynamics of black time must be recognized as different from that of contemporary mainstream Western culture.[5]

The Vertical Technique allows one to analyze *Cane* as a reorganization of history. As an analytical tool, it redistributes time to show the impact of understanding the African-American point of view. The Incursion Cycle focuses on abnormalities that challenge the elements stabilizing the culture. Karintha is the "November Cotton Flower," a literary Dorothy Dandridge. She is a "desperate" beauty born out of season, unexpected and misunderstood. Her existence presents tortuous questions. What place does a beautiful African-American woman or child occupy in America in 1923? What place can she hope to occupy beyond 1923?

Karintha is supposed to already know her place as a child, but she doesn't. That is why she keeps overstepping the boundaries set by her environment for her. Once she has completed the maturation cycle—from sensuous childhood through promiscuous adolescence to wanton adulthood—she begins to act more "normal." Men bring her gifts in exchange for her affection and access to her body. Karintha marries nameless men, who do not understand their participation in the debasement of her innocence as a human being. Houston A. Baker notes in *Singers of Daybreak: Studies in Black American Literature* that when black women are considered property (in literature or real life) deep relationships are impossible. So Karintha becomes a different kind of incursion against her environment. Beauty bought, she commands the power that women are taught to dream about. Her description is Toomer's first attempt to bring together the temporal and the nontemporal. Karintha is a woman, a human being, a concrete entity in the world. She carries perfect, ethereal beauty and a soul that was ripened too soon; which like the sunset, exist as nontemporal entities.

> *Karintha* carrying *beauty, perfect* as dusk when the sun goes down ... *Karintha*, at twelve was a *wild flash ... Karintha* is a woman. Men do not know *that the soul of her* was a growing thing *ripened too soon. Karintha* at twenty, carrying *beauty, perfect* as dusk when the *sun goes down.*

The repetition and the simile are a penitential psalm/chant (a blues song) of praise that loses its impact in Georgia in 1923.

"Reapers" and "November Cotton Flower" continue the attack on the culture and the land that "Karintha" has initiated. The African-American reapers are described as medieval icons of death—an appropriate image for those who help to corrupt her life.[6] They are reaping the legacy of slaughter that is so much a part of the South's history. Meanwhile, the November Cotton Flower, as an omen, predicts the continued withering away of the land and the culture.

The advent of Becky poses a major threat to the tradition of southern gentility, which legislated the separation of the Africans from Europeans and Euro-Americans as early as the seventeenth century. The punishment of death or ostracism for any "white woman" willingly having conjugal relationships with a black man provides a measure of how revolutionary Becky's attitude was in 1923. (In accordance with the law, there is no punishment for "white men or white women" having sex with black women.) She not only appears to chose to have sex with an African-

American man (at least twice), she chooses on both occasions to bear the children conceived by those illicit relationships rather than to abort them. (We know abortion was a possible alternative because Karintha previously aborted a child in the forest and then burned it.)

While she is ostracized, she is not killed, and she lives to see the manhood of her two boy children, who curse "the white folks and curse the niggers" and leave town. Becky's behavior acts as an acid to wear away the substance of separatist indoctrination in the South. She also participates in establishing a new class that will have to create new laws for everyone, since the existing laws for Euro-Americans or African-Americans will not be applicable. Becky will not verify, justify, or rationalize the appropriateness of segregation by being assimilated into the Euro-American southern genteel tradition, and the African-American man or men who have "collaborated" with her do not offer themselves as scapegoats for the society. Southern society will have to face its worst nightmare and decide what to do with the man or men who have acted against their sacred beliefs in the present (in 1923) and who may act against them in the future—in the form of Becky's boys.

Although the southern genteel tradition advocates racial purity and abhors miscegenation (beyond the economic function of creating more slaves as workers), the sociosexual politics of slavery encouraged a subconscious desire for interracial relationships. This tradition, Houston A. Baker insists in *Singers of Daybreak*, makes a penitential ritual necessary. He says Becky is a shaman who has the ability to enable the community to act out its abnormalities and to reinforce its capacity to resist abnormal behavior. Because she has engaged in public taboo behavior, other members of the society can see their behavior mirrored in her, and she can be the cause of a dialogue around why they engage in it and then devalue that engagement. Simultaneously, she serves as a model for why they should resist "interracial intercourse" because she is seen as a pariah who is ostracized on an "eye-shaped piece of sandy ground" between the road and the railroad tracks. Everyone can see her punishment. Her discomfort in living on land on which she can't even grow anything is visual evidence arguing that the genteel tradition must be upheld and no Euro-American woman should have sex with African-American men.

The following poem, "Face," shows the effects of the Incursion Cycle on Becky. It is a woman's aged hair, worn face, and worker's body (channeled muscles) that are under attack, as Becky's body is left deteriorating under the collapsed chimney and "nearly ripe for worms."

"Cotton Song" is the first of four songs in *Cane* that sets the tone for the agrarian folk culture that is disappearing with the birth of mechanized industry in America. "Cotton Song" paints the lush countryside and the bale-rolling days of Africana men and women. It is a work song that records the "weary sinner's bare feet trod" and describes the environment in which Carma is as strong as a man and in which her husband, Bane, must leave home to find work. Carma is the final attack on the role of Africana women in the southern genteel tradition. Her participation was crucial in the construction and maintenance of that tradition during slavery and afterwards. Houston Baker says that Carma "can hardly be said to possess a strong sense of responsibility."[7] However, if the reader assumes Carma is acting intentionally and intelligently (out of some comprehensible motive), she can accept the concept of Carma having taking responsibility for herself to act out her sexuality in a way that contradicts the southern genteel tradition. Carma is not a southern belle, like Karintha, or a mother's martyr, like Becky. She is a physically strong, healthy, sexy woman who is not afraid of men because she is as strong as they are. This unusual combination of attributes presents an anomaly, to say the least. Carma is not just abnormal in the southern tradition; she also does not represent the attitude and physiology of any of the well-known feminine stereotypes inhabiting elite American literature. Those stereotypes include: The Fair Virgin, The Siren, The Mother, The Seductress, The Priestess, The Prim Little Lady, The Tragic Mulatto, The Pariah, The Liberated Woman, The Temptress, The Gossip, The Old Maid, The Housewife/Matron, The White Temptress, and The Sexual Object.

Carma resembles the Mafo, or the Mother of the Fong of the Bamileke tribe in South Cameroon. The Mafo is regarded as an equivalent of the chief in Fong society. Their hierarchical structure resembles the Coniagui as an exogamous matrilineal tribe in West Africa. Among the Coniagui, it is through the mother that family identity, privileges of rank, material possession, and political power are allocated to the line of descendants.

> She is afforded the same rites as the chief at her death and exercises complete control of her life and the lives of all the other women in the community, which means she controls all the agriculture and partakes of the profit from the commerce of the tribe. Dressed in traditional masculine attire the Mafo participates in the decision making of the administrative council, where it is said she takes precedence over the chief. She has her own property, may choose a husband while retaining the right to sexually enjoy other men. She retains complete immunity from any authority. She presides over the women's secret societies and participates in those of the men unless they are of military nature.[8]

In fact, Toomer's third-person omniscient narrator tells the reader that Carma is a part of a legacy that is not solely American.

She does not sing; her body is a song. She is in the forest, dancing. Torches flare ... juju men, greegree, witch-doctors ... torches go out ... the Dixie Pike has grown from a goat path in Africa.[9]

Understandably, Bane (a poison, a cause of trouble, misery, or anxiety) is a foil of Carma (karma—the East Indian Buddhist concept of a person's actions in successive existences), and their relationship becomes "melo-dramatic." Bane accuses her of infidelity but cannot physically beat her (in the male tradition of dispensing punishment) because she is as strong as he is. Hence tradition is further eroded. His masculinity is challenged at its most essential level. Unable to punish Carma for deceiving him twice, Bane slashes a man who helped him moments before. The result is indeed melodramatic, as Bane is sentenced to work on the prison chain gang as punishment for slashing the man who helped him. The incursion has been successful. The society and culture are not as strong as they were previously.

There are only hints of what is wrong until "Song of the Son" appears next in the text. As the second song in *Cane*, it is a lament, not a work song. For the first time, the reader gets a clear view of the consciousness that is telling the story of the Georgia countryside in 1923. In this poem, Charles Davis writes eloquently:

> We are introduced to the consciousness of a poet-speaker who imposes unity upon the verses, sketches, narratives, and symbolic signs that make up the body of the work.
>
> "Song of the Son" describes a return to a scene from which the poet has long been separated ...
>
> > "Pour O pour that parting soul in song,
> > O pour it in the saw dust glow of night,
> > Into the Velvet pine-smoke air tonight,
> > And let the valley carry it along,
> > And let the valley carry it along."
>
> What is at stake is not merely the desire for physical delight, though this is strong; the poet realizes that he is responding to "that parting soul," the spirit in the land. The reference to "parting" introduces the problem of time. The poet has returned "just before an epoch's sun declines," at the moment when the land is losing a value that it has long possessed ... The poet has returned in time to secure possession of one vestige of the old culture, one "plum" providing the seed that would enable him to reconstruct the earlier civilization. This is important to do because of the ancient beauty that becomes now available to him and because the new awareness forms a basis for new songs, to be created, no doubt by the poet ...
>
> "Song of the Son" presents the consciousness that stands behind the varied verbal structures in *Cane*. In the poem it is a sophisticated intelligence yearning for

the completion and adequate expression and finding the means for achieving these ends in contact with the South and with a newly discovered black culture.[10]

Elsewhere in *Cane*, Davis notes, this consciousness becomes a sympathetic narrator (in "Karintha" and "Carma," for example) who provides an "intellectual context" for the stories or a curious "I" (in "Becky" and "Fern") who wonders at the "mysteries and contradictions of Southern life."

The poem "Georgia Dusk" is a portrait of sundown in the atrophying world of *Cane*. The beauty and the languid indolence the portrait reflects are repeated in the characterizations of women to come in *Cane*, who are all "canefield concubines" surrounded by "men with vestiges of pomp."

Fernie Mae Rosen is the first of those beautiful, indolent, incomprehensible women in the Atrophy Cycle in *Cane*. Like Karintha, Becky, and Carma, Fern represents an abnormality in the Georgia countryside, but she doesn't have the energy and drive that the other women have. None of the women in the Atrophy and Destruction Cycles have that kind of energy. Fern clearly presents the developing narrator's ambiguous attitudes toward race. This ambiguity about racial identity and racial responsibility is one of the elements undermining the culture and the society. The mulatto class, out of slavery, confuses the issue of segregation because they are neither Euro-American or African-American: Rather, they are African-Euro-American, without land to stabilize their identities. That dilemma becomes clear when the Vertical Technique is used to analyze the structure of *Cane*. Chris Antoinides notes in an abstract of his study *Jean Toomer: The Burden of Impotent Pain*:

> What emerges from the cumulative weight of the exegesis is that *Cane* is far more congruent with Toomer's ambiguous attitudes toward race than has been formerly thought. Through an elaborate permutation and combination of significant imagery, tone and motifs, Toomer's book does not simply affirm the theme of racial resurgence as posited in the Harlem Renaissance. Rather, it celebrates the Negro's past glories in a degenerating present, and affirms the absorption of the black race by the white.[11]

Fern is an African-Jewish American, as Hargis Westerfield points out in "Jean Toomer's Fern: A Mythical Dimension."

> Besides the name Rosen, unmistakable Jewish references occur again and again. Five sentences from the start, Toomer says, "Her nose was aquiline, Semitic." In the next sentence, he says that if one has heard a Jewish cantor sing, he will know the narrator's feelings, when he looks at her face (p. 24). Later, our narrator says that at first sight of her, he felt as if he had heard a Jewish cantor sing (p.

28). And in the epiphany where Fern rejects carnal love, she sings like a "Jewish cantor singing with a broken voice" (p. 32). Such are Toomer's plainly Jewish references.[12]

Fern is not one of the three ethnicities but all three amalgamated. Toomer emphasizes her Jewishness. She is also a spiritualist and a woman. Her essential nature, as reflected in her eyes, seems to "hold God." Toomer merges the temporal and the nontemporal in Fern to suggest the mishandling of the extraordinary complexity of woman as cosmic entity. Westerfield believes that Fern's Jewishness is an attempt to define her as a descendant of Mary, mother of Jesus, and thus, insist upon her holiness—her sacredness of person—despite her Africana identity that also connects her to other Biblical women who struggled to actualize the nature of their spirituality: (such as Theodora—AD 100-200; Perpetua—AD 150-200; Monica, the mother of Saint Augustine—AD 354-430; and Zipporah, the wife of Moses).

Fern is atrophy personified except when she is having a mystical experience—intercourse with God. Other than that, she appears listless, empty, atrophied, but astonishingly beautiful and sensual. In the same way, the poem "Nullo" (null or having no legal force amounting to nothing) reflects a deadly silence at dusk. It is a stillness that is generated by—not imposed upon—the world of *Cane*. As Bernard Bell argues in "A Key to the Poems in *Cane*," this study insists that the songs and poems are all functional.

> Contrary to Professor Turner's observation, none of the fifteen poems in Parts One and Two are "exquisite only in the sharpness and suggestiveness of their imagery." They are all functional, serving to elucidate or to set the stage or to provide a transition between the sketches.[13]

"Nullo"'s stillness is, in fact, a prelude to Esther's nothingness. "Her cheeks are too flat and dead for a girl of nine." "Nullo" predicts the depiction of her physical and psychological atrophy as the cycle continues to unfold.

In contrast, "Evening Song" is a love song in the order of romantic ballads. It portrays a woman, Cloine, waiting with "her lips apart," a double sexual image suggesting that she awaits a lover who will kiss one pair of her lips and enter the doorway marked by the second pair of open lips. Cloine tires and sleeps where she dreams of meeting the narrator/lover, with "lips pressed against her heart." Figuratively, it is the story of Esther's tragedy condensed into a tale of unrequited love and longing.

Edward E. Waldron begins his analysis of "Esther" in "The Search for Identity in Jean Toomer's Esther"[14] by refuting Robert Bone's analysis of it in *The Negro Novel in America*[15] "as a tale of a frigid girl's longing for the open masculinity of 'King Barlo,' her subsequent failure to give herself to him, and her return to frigidity." A more text-based reading of the action would involve an emotionally and physically isolated young woman's attempt to establish a relationship with a man who sees himself separated from her by class (she's the daughter of the richest colored man in town) and caste (she is described as having milk-white skin).

One major theme in "Esther" deals with the relationship of the light-skinned African-American to the rest of the Africana community in which he or she must try to function. The second major theme, also common to the Harlem Renaissance, is the relationship between the African-American and Africa. Esther is set above most of the members in the African-American community by her color and her father's membership in the merchant class. However, her isolation has left her alone at all levels, to the point of becoming neurotic. She is educated but has no life to support her development as a person intellectually or socially. When she goes to "pick Barlo up" at a local bordello, the people there taunt her about being "dictie." Barlo tells her where he is is no place for her to be. Waldron says that Esther rejects Barlo's earthy primitiveness and in rejecting Barlo, she rejects the strange lost world that is Africa. A more careful reading of the text suggests just the opposite—that Barlo rejects what she offers him (symbolized by her class and caste) as a way of holding on to his powerful connection to Africa, confirmed in his historic preached text within the story.

The reader may ask whether this means that Toomer saw the "American Negro" as the hopeless victim of circumstance, caught in limbo, without a country or a culture. How he structures text and defines place through imagery suggests otherwise. However, "Esther" does suggest that the search for an identity (when it denies reality in favor of a more attractive and less painful dream) is doomed to achieve either nothing or madness. Every human being is limited by his or her conceptual realities. The question is whether one accepts them and works to expand them to mold one's own identity or whether one chooses Esther's route to escape reality and chase after futile dreams. Toomer's ultimate answer is that we are all human. Unfortunately, both Toomer and Esther lived in a society that would not allow them the dignity of being just a member of the human race. Denied of her dignity, Esther is at her mental or physical death even more pallid and desiccated than Becky, says Odette C. Martin in "*Cane:* Method and Myth." Whether the reader agrees with this study—suggesting that Esther does not die but goes mad—or Martin, who says she died physically, it is clear that Esther continues the Atrophy Cycle with images of powerful biblical symbolism and dissipation.

Esther makes the most meaningful statement up to this point in *Cane* of the American experience for Toomer as a "black man." It affirms that the principles of whiteness, a metaphor for physical and spiritual devitalization and materialism and maleness that is aggression which have long battered the female principle, now corrupt the black male [principle] ...

But Barlo's inadequacies are matched by Esther's. She is afraid of her own sexuality and wants an infant "immaculately" conceived. As the potential madonna (an enfeebled America), she lacks sufficient vitality, except at the level of her own fantasies, to rescue, through love and giving birth, a blackness which is not only blighted but debauched. The surrealistic fiction of "Esther" offers a first clue to one of the directions that Parts II, and especially III, will take, the need for messiah, man or child, who will deliver, not only blacks, but America too.[16]

The reader can interpret Esther's willingness to go get Barlo as evidence against an analysis of her personality as nonsexual or not wanting to engage in coitus. What takes her so long to go is a matter related to complex social conditioning related to caste and class—not desire.

The savior to deliver African-Americans and America will not be the Barlo described in the next poem called "Conversion." As Bell notes in "A Key to the Poems in *Cane*," "Conversion" heightens the meaning of the parable in Barlo's sermon by exposing the Christian deception of substituting a white-faced sardonic God for the "African Guardian of Souls." The poem also provides a fitting ending to the Atrophy Cycle. The religion of the African was his life's philosophy, the basis of his culture and society. Unlike the European concept of Christianity, for the African it held the functional worldview around which he ordered his everyday interaction. In "Conversion" the necessity of maintaining Western domination over African-Americans is made obvious, as the African's original religious construct is supplanted and another is substituted in its place. It is a bell of doom for the culture and the people that use it to define reality.

Most importantly, traditional African religious philosophy provided a code of morality that was not negotiable. For instance, it could not hold the mutually incompatible concepts of debasing the human body (the house of the ancestors) while forwarding the well-being of the tribe. The debasement of human beings was not a part of the traditional African concept of slavery (not chattel ownership), where the extended family was used to provide work, education, and a home for many, many people. In fact, much of what caused Africans to be dominated by European powers in the eighteenth, nineteenth, and twentieth centuries is a reluctance to develop a hostile attitude toward the human body. This reverence translates into a reluctance to kill Euro-Americans that only in recent times has been overcome. Two striking Africana poetic examples of extraordinary literature clearly advocating violence (as a response to oppression) are

Keorapetse Kgositsile's *The Present Is a Very Dangerous Place to Live* and Stanley Crouch's *Ain't No Ambulance for No Nigguhs Tonight.*

The poem "Portrait in Georgia" confirms the bell of doom coming, as it introduces the Destruction Cycle with negative images of woman as the culture carrier. Her whole body is described as an embodiment of death—that is, metaphorically "white as the ash of black flesh after flame." Toomer uses the poem to foreshadow a lynching that will involve a woman in the Destruction Cycle.[17] However, the title of the poem tells us that he is painting a picture of a lifestyle, both in the poem and in the work that follows it. Even if the work seems to be too "artistic" to be true, the reader should be properly warned not to discredit what he reads as imaginary. Like the painter transferring the live images to canvas, Toomer has transferred the sights and sounds of the lives of African-Americans, as he experienced them, to *Cane*.

"Blood-Burning Moon," or the tragedy of Louisa, opens the Destruction Cycle. The story revolves around Bob Stone, a Euro-American man, and Tom Burwell, an African-American man who—in the southern dueling tradition—fight to the death over the exclusive possession of the beautiful and talented African-American country maiden, Louisa. Bob Stone feels an incomprehensible attraction toward her, whom he finds lovely in a "nigger way." He establishes the fact of their sexual relationship within the story. Tom Burwell adores his fiancée Louisa because she is the epitome of everything that he considers beautiful and pure. He intimates that he has not had coitus with her, having decided to wait until he proposes marriage. Tom settles instead on listening to her sing in her lyrical voice. Though the two men destroy each other in an attempt to possess Louisa, the destruction theme extends to other levels in the story.

> In this story, the conflict is not racial, but even more primitive. Animal, irrational forces, symbolized in the blood-burning moon, "the full moon, an evil thing," involve two men for the possession of a woman. On another symbolic level, the story points toward the slow surrender of both the white and the Negro male to the destructive civilization of the North. Neither Bob, whose family was once so wealthy that the men could have all the female slaves they wanted, but whose fortune has been swallowed by modern industrialism; nor Tom, "from factory town," can truly possess Louisa, a symbol of the land.[18]

Perhaps the real cause of the tragedy is Louisa's ambivalence to the situation at the beginning of the narrative and her announced desire to possess both men as a woman's right to choose her lover—reminiscent of Carma's dilemma. Nevertheless, the nature of the racial conflict in "Blood-Burning Moon" adds the necessary political element that makes *Cane* a uniquely American literary work. Louisa, like Carma, has two men in love with her. Because of their combined attention and resources, Louisa enjoys a rare advantage as a neo-southern belle in Georgia in 1923. Understandably, she does not wish to choose between them. Whereas life as Tom Burwell's sharecropper wife will not compare to her present independent status as a single woman who works, neither will an endless, illicit affair with neo-planter Bob Stone (who cannot marry her under the laws of Georgia) be as satisfying or provide protection for any children that she might have. Nevertheless, Louisa fails to see the necessity of making a choice, under the political sociopolitical law that governs all actions in the South in 1923. In avoiding this necessity, Patricia Chase in "The Women in *Cane*" says Louisa ignores the price that must be paid for pitting the manhood of an African-American and Euro-American against each other.

> Lulled by the heat, the heavy, sweet scent of sugar cane, which carries the aura of death and violence, as well as love, and drugged by the "blood-burning" moon, Louisa has not considered the effects of her actions in the light of her environment and the ways of men. She lives, like many of Toomer's women, in the here and now ... She is young and reckless, which is youth's gift. Thus how can she comprehend when the past crashes together with the present before her? Not wishing to choose between Tom and Bob, and in her glory, she has forgotten the pride of men.[19]

Aside from the personal and political levels of destruction in "Blood-Burning Moon," the reader is faced with symbolic destruction or cosmic distress. Louise Blackwell in "Jean Toomer's *Cane* and Biblical Myth" reminds us that the sun stands for Christ, the moon is the eye of God, clouds symbolize the presence of God, and the red moon is frequently used to symbolize the Host drenched in his own blood. In "Blood-Burning Moon" we find numerous lines referring to the nature of planetary presence signaling something auspicious about to happen. The red moon has often been called the Harvest Moon based on the time of year it rises and changes color, and the longitudinal position of the viewer. The system of racism harvests Tom and Bob for their mutual arrogance in assuming powers they cannot possibly possess in America in 1923.

The Bible's documentation of its many pagan rituals includes Louise Blackwell's notation of both human and animal sacrifices occurring under certain forms of the moon. In "Blood-Burning Moon" Toomer uses Louisa to sacrifice two men representing their separate ethnic groups to the god of progress. Neither of these two male archetypes, The Southern Planter or The Black Buck, can continue to exist as they are in America in 1923. Toomer sacrifices them to ensure the success of the Great Migration North, where African-American people think that they will find a new order, a new world in a new vision of America.

Symbolically, Tom Burwell is a Christ-figure and the bloody moon a sign of the Day of Judgement, the time when man will be judged for his inhumanity to man. Each of the three parts of the sketch conclude with a lyrical refrain to the moon. Louisa's thoughts dominate the first [section], Tom's the second, and Bob's the third. The image of the full blood-red moon looms large and ominously over the action of each part. And the title of the sketch alludes to the Book of Revelation 6:12: "And I beheld when he had opened the sixth seal, and lo, there was a great earthquake: and the sun became black as sack cloth of hair, and the moon became as blood."[20]

Assuming American racism is the modern-day Antichrist in Blackwell's construct, then the wrath of God, *Cane* suggests, will fall heavy on those who have sought and still seek to frustrate the will to harmonize man, God, and nature—the inherited focus of traditional African philosophy.

Like the other imagistic sketches in the Incursion and Atrophy Cycles, the intricate pattern of myth, symbol, and song in "Blood-Burning Moon" focuses on the conflict between natural impulses and social conventions.

In "Portrait of the Artist as the High Priest of Soul," Bernard Bell questions the inherent dialectic that *Cane*'s women struggle to resolve. "As the narrator passes through the rural South, he bears witness to women—symbolized as the principle of receptivity and fertility—attempting to harmonize their physical drives with the psychic centers of their being and with the male principle.[21] It is an impossible task in Georgia, where African-American men, women, and children were put at risk in the state's system of instant justice.

The Crisis chronicles Georgia's rise as the empire state of lynching by 1923. More African-American men and women were lynched in Georgia than in any other state, as indicated in figures 2.3, 2.4, and 2.5.

President Wilson's declaration on the matter in 1919 shows that lynching had become enough of a problem to attract national attention. In "Blood-Burning Moon" Toomer is not just making a comment about the laws of the American antebellum period, but also about the nature of justice and predicting how those laws would haunt us in modern times with incidents like the lynch dragging in Jasper, Texas. There could be no justice in the South in 1923. The African-American response would be to go north in the biggest recorded voluntary population shift in American history.

After killing the pastoral vision of life under southern gentility in the Incursion and Atrophy cycles of *Cane*, Toomer moves the setting to Washington, D.C., and presents in "Seventh Street" a candid and vivid description of life on the African-American "strip" in 1923 and during Prohibition, after the war. "Seventh Street" establishes a literary transition to orient the reader to a new place with the same problems camouflaged

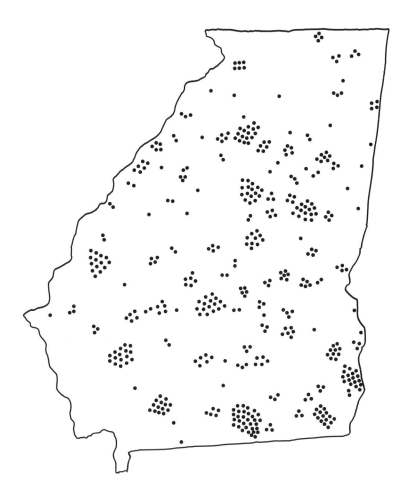

A Map of Georgia, The Empire State
of Lynching, identifying the sites of 460
persons lynched between 1835 and 1920.
The location of each lynching is approximate, since many have occurred in the
same places.

▶ **Figure 2.3 Georgia: The Empire State of Lynching.** "The Lynching Industry,
1920" (M. G. Allison), *Crisis* 21, no. 4 (February 1921), pp. 160–168.
Drawn by M. G. Allison.

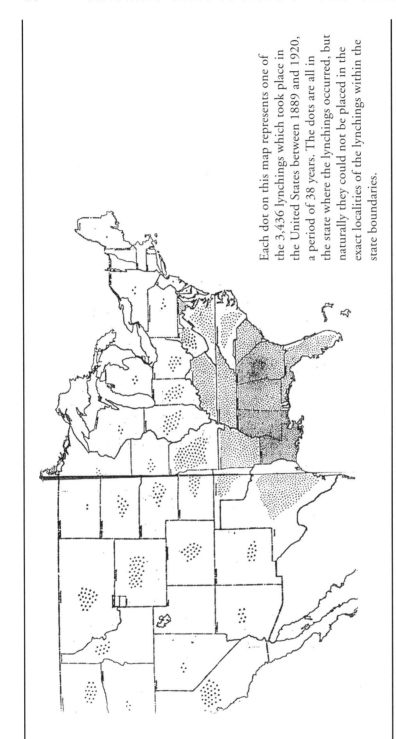

Each dot on this map represents one of the 3,436 lynchings which took place in the United States between 1889 and 1920, a period of 38 years. The dots are all in the state where the lynchings occurred, but naturally they could not be placed in the exact localities of the lynchings within the state boundaries.

▲ **Figure 2.4 A Lynching Map of the United States.** "The Lynching Industry, 1920" (M. G. Allison) *Crisis* 21, no. 4 (February 1921), pp. 160–168. Drawn by M. G. Allison.

HELP CRUSH OUT LYNCHING

The Anti-Lynching Committee of the N. A. A. C. P. earnestly
appeals for contributions to its Anti-Lynching Fund—no matter how little, or much—to back President Wilson's crusade
against lynching—the monster disloyalty to America.

> " I say plainly that every American who takes part in the
> action of a mob or gives any sort of countenance is no
> true son of this great democracy, but its betrayer, and does
> more to discredit her by that single disloyalty to her stand-
> ards of law and right than the words of her statesmen or
> sacrifices of her heroic soldiers in the trenches can do to
> make a suffering people believe in her, their savior."
> —*From President Wilson's Lynching
> and Mob Violence Pronouncement.*

President Wilson's appeal must be heeded.   The suppression of
lynching has become a test of national patriotism.   Lynching per-
sists because those who practice it believe in it more strongly than the
opponents of lynching believe in "ordered law and humane justice."

Eight Negroes were lynched in the ten weeks following the President's pronouncement.   No one was arrested or put on trial because
of these lynchings.

Every lynching must be investigated.   The facts must be brought
home to the people of America.   Governors must be appealed to in
each specific case to uphold the law.   (The punishment of lynchers
has been held to be an affair of local authorities in the States.)   The
pressure of national condemnation must be brought to bear upon
local authorities everywhere.   Public opinion must be aroused until
it becomes a vital and compelling force.   The public conscience must
be stimulated to decisive action.   When aroused, this awakened conscience must be organized, vitalized and centred upon effective means
of action.

▶ **Figure 2.5 *Crisis* Anti-Lynching Ad.** "Help Crush Out Lynching," *Crisis* 17, no.
3 (January 1919) back cover.

▲ **Figure 2.6 Karintha as a Child.** *Cane.* St. Louis Community College production, April 1978. Photo: Brian Gordon

▶ **Figure 2.7 The Narrator and a Fainting Fernie Mae Rose.** *Cane.*
St. Louis Community College production, April 1978.
Photo: Brian GordonPhoto: Brian Gordon

▶ **Figure 2.8 Bob Stone.** *Cane.* St. Louis Community College
production, April 1978. Photo: Brian Gordon

▶ **Figure 2.9 Tom Burwell.** *Cane.* St. Louis Community College production, April 1978. Photo: Brian Gordon

▶ **Figure 2.10 The Narrator and Avey.** *Cane.* St. Louis Community College production, April 1978. Photo: Brian Gordon

▶ **Figure 2.11 Bona and Paul.** *Cane.* St. Louis Community College production, April 1978. Photo: Brian Gordon

▲ **Figure 2.12 Scene from Kabnis—The Party.** *Cane.* St. Louis Community College production, April 1978. Photo: Brian Gordon

▶ **Figure 2.13 Kabnis and Carrie Kate.** *Cane.* St. Louis Community College production, April 1978. Photo: Brian Gordon

differently. Cancel says in "Male and Female Interrelationships in Toomer's *Cane*" that Toomer uses "Seventh Street" to establish the main conflict of *Cane* as the dissipation and corruption of African-American dignity through the application of capitalism to a people who are fundamentally socialist. "Seventh Street" is an introduction to seeing what happened to the "Factr'y Town" inhabitants who moved north because the myth of black life under slavery and neoslavery (sharecropping) was destroyed.

All concepts of wealth in the South center on owning land. In the North that concept gets translated into owning a house. "Rhobert" is the first person that we meet who demonstrates the North's unsuccessful function as a foil for southern society's demarcations and frustrations.

Rhobert as a robot is as dead as the house he wears on his head, as he thinks about it and organizes his life around it. The house is not a symbol of wealth in his case; rather, it is symbol of his and society's obsession with African-American petty bourgeois materialism under segregation. Rhobert's true purpose and will as a human being are "being drawn off" like water, as he remains misdirected and nonproductive.

God, like the white-faced sardonic god in "Conversion," is "a Red-Cross man with a dredge and a respiration-pump who's waiting for you at the opposite periphery." God built the house, like he made everything else in the Christian ontology. Rhobert's attempt to possess the house (like land in the South) is futile. Land, in the African ontological structure, cannot be owned—only used. Rhobert does not understand this principle as he abandons his wife and children in the South to become the slave of a house, in a segregated neighborhood in Washington, D.C. He is on a path to a sad death where no happy going-home songs will celebrate his funeral. The mourners will sing the Negro spiritual born in slavery's darkness, "Deep River," as they lay him, as a destroyed man, in the grave.

> "Deep River, My home is over Jordan
> Deep River, I want to cross over into campground"

The destruction of Avey is a more complicated affair. She is the first woman in the urban section of the Destruction Cycle, and as such she provides a way of revealing the destructive northern forces, which include the city as a metaphor for the principles of Eurocentric thought, materialism, puritanical Christianity, and modern (scientific) rationality. Viewing "Avey" through the Vertical Technique reveals the nature of her dual reality, as an educated woman who failed to achieve the ultimate integration of self and society. Like the women who come before her in *Cane* (but for different reasons), she is an orphan, standing outside of both of her societies—African-American and Euro-American.

As a Negro "orphan-woman" in 1923, Avey symbolizes, as William J. Goede points out in "Jean Toomer's Ralph Kabnis: Portrait of the Negro Artist as a Young Man," the fertility of the African-American soul. The narrator loves her, but she does not pay attention to him. Like Karintha, she passes from innocence to awareness of her womanhood to corruption in a world where African-Americans cannot determine their future as a community. At first, she has intercourse with a college student, whom she visits in his flat. She never reciprocates the narrator's infatuation with her. However, like the other previous males, he cannot fathom the mystery of the female soul because he continually objectifies her. Failing to perceive her real need, he mistakes her indifference for indolence. He cannot understand that, unlike the other, earlier females, Avey is displaced. Like Rhobert, she belongs to the South, to the soil of which she is a mere extension in *Cane*. In 1923, in New York or in Washington, D.C., the "Negro" female loses her dignity and sensibility in a competition to enter mainstream thought or culture where she is a second-class citizen; without changing her economic condition she has no hope of changing her status. The sophisticated narrator, a product of northern civilization, does not comprehend that Avey is orphaned from her intellect, her talent, her self-development. Her life is artistically destroyed; it maintains its form without apparent significant content.

Avey transcends the states of the women in the Incursion and Atrophy Cycles of *Cane* by embodying at least one problem that each of them have. Her strong link to the earth through her body makes her respond instinctively to life. The effect is that she is a composite character reminding the reader of each of the previous female characters in some way. She avoids the personal destruction that the earlier women experience by living a dissipated life in an urban environment, thereby illustrating a new way of manifesting death in *Cane*. Avey will neither agree to pursue the god of materialism like Rhobert nor try to force the environment to recognize her in some professional manner. She will simply be unattached, unowned, unpossessed—an orphan who is a woman that is no one's victim.

The existence of this null or "Nullo" life that Avey settles for is reinforced by the poem "Beehive." The busy bee, as a physical metaphor for mankind, seems aptly applied to Avey's Washington, D.C., federal government population, which at 8:00 A.M. and 5:00 P.M. looks like a swarm of bees. More importantly, "Beehive" depicts the null life (that Avey chooses or falls prey to) as being equivalent to the mass-mind activity of bees accepting their worker function within the collective without questions or struggle. Toomer's imagery says when man fails to develop his intellectual and spiritual capacities, when he does not pursue continued enlightenment and progessive evolution, he is no more than a sterile drone going through the actions of being alive. "Beehive" also foreshadows the chaotic emptiness of John in "Theater." The vibrancy of Dorris's dance as an African-American art form is a silver honey on which he gets drunk. Being a drunk drone, he can then "wish to fly out past the moon and curl forever in some far-off farmyard flower" in the land of "dreamed fluted cane."

"Storm Ending" contrasts the beauty and power of different aspects of nature and poses the irreconcilable dialectic in the sweet earth flying from the fierce thunder, that man neither understands nor appreciates. Nature's domain extends beyond the land of dream-fluted cane. The beauty and power of nature in the thunder, in the flowers, in the wind, in the sun, in the rain can be seen anywhere that the conscious mind looks to find them. When man becomes oblivious to nature, he has killed an important aspect of his own being. John has annihilated his ability to think and act. He lives in the life of his thoughts.

In "Theater" the reader sees the action through Dorris's dance, John's dialogue with Mame, and his stream-of-consciousness dialogue with himself. Dorris and Mame are chorus girls who have found John, the manager's brother, a likely candidate for lover. However, John is no longer able to actively respond to the power of woman as a natural part of the beauty and power of nature. His response is intellectual and singly shared with himself. John is a twentieth-century urbanized professional, who has been taught by capitalism to keep his personal life separate from his professional life. He knows that he will not have any kind of meaningful interaction with Dorris. Nevertheless, his mind cannot resist the seductive power of the dance. Like Avey's would-be lover, he talks to himself. In this context George Kopf's description of Toomer's methodology in "The Tensions in Jean Toomer's Theater" describes Toomer's methodology for developing characters.

> Toomer's characterization is not the objective product of a sequence of fictive development within the story, but represents, instead, given values which he brings to the story.[22]

John represents the problem of living as a single isolated mind, and Dorris represents the problem of living with superfluous emotions.

Kopf discusses Toomer's anthropomorphizing without noticing John's lack of motion and emotion and Dorris's inability to use the power of the dance to move him. Although she impresses the manager and the assorted watchers seeking asylum from the "nigger alleys" that surround the Howard Theater, it isn't enough. Dorris has redefined herself and her dance. The dance becomes a medium of barter for John's attention and success, in the mode of the classical American Dream. The dance, which is her true self, appears to be a "dead thing" to John's unresponsive humanity. It is also a "dead thing" to her later because of its failure to get John to move toward her and into her life. She is distraught, diminished, dispirited, and destroyed emotionally at the end of the scenario—though not driven insane like Esther. The difference is in Dorris's having a seasoned mentor, while Esther is completely isolated from all functional feminine networks. Mame had warned Dorris earlier. "Told you nothin doing" is what Mame says to comfort her.

"Her Lips Are Copper Wire" equates the process of communicating artificially, with a phone, to the transmission of power through the medium of the human mouth. When human communication is successful, the result is illuminating or electrifying. The mechanical version is empty in comparison—though expedient across distances. The discussion of the kiss as a transmission of spirit will be important to remember in "Box Seat."

"Calling Jesus" is an introduction to the character of Muriel in "Box Seat." Her soul is like a little thrust-tailed dog that follows her whimpering. Without her soul, she is superficial, without substance and without power. "Calling Jesus" emphasizes the theme of the female soul being oppressed by the environment of the North in the Destruction Cycle. Stifled in her surroundings, her soul yearns for the "clean hay cut" and the "dream-fluted cane" of the South's landscape. Her soul calls to Jesus, as does Becky's, for salvation; yet salvation lies not in the oppressive North, but in the South where Cancel says, "the bare feet of Christ move across bales of Southern cotton."

Dan Moore, Muriel's ardent admirer, is portrayed as the King Barlo of the North. He can feel spiritual change coming. He knows that he and Muriel have been separated from something essential that they need to survive, and he struggles to get her to understand and name the unconscious element that is missing. Their environment is portrayed as artificial. The houses are sharp-edged metallic with cold walls. The theater seats are metal slots that help them sit upright. With Mrs. Pribby's help, Muriel hopes to attain the rewards of respectability, but the text questions whether or not it is possible in a perverse environment.

Whereas all of *Cane* exposes Toomer's concern with the preoccupations of the divisions of race and class, which disrupt the unity of body and soul in twentieth-century life, "Box Seat" seems to be *Cane*'s most concise dramatic expression of Toomer's desire for a profound healing.

Elizabeth Schultz in "Jean Toomer's 'Box Seat:' The Possibility for 'Constructive Crisis,'" describes it as Toomer's yearning for the antagonisms of race, class, and the separation of body and soul to be healed.[23] Toomer sees the potential for negation or destruction of all of these elements and the person, if balance is not achieved.

Dan succumbs to the anesthetic effect of inaction toward all the implying traumas. He is not physically destroyed but he is certainly ineffectual or null, as the poem "Prayer" describes. Like his mind, Dan's body is opaque to the soul. He is weak at the end of "Box Seat," not the dynamo imbued with power that he imagines he is during the story. The events of the story have left him so weak that he has confused the body with the soul; confused the state of the world, confused about the reasons why Muriel is the way he is. Dan—like Muriel, John, Dorris, and Avey—is trapped in a limbo existence that perfectly balances nothingness and death in an urban segregated society.

Death, in the city, has so many faces, and as "Harvest Song" suggests, the grim reaper extracts his price by not taking men's bodies but instead their souls. Nothingness is a terrifying death to experience.[24] The hunger for substance and power in the human spirit is a powerful metaphor for life itself; Toomer's reaper is blind but sees, is deaf but hears, has food but cannot consume it. He is a metaphor for the condition of the African-American's invisible status in American society in 1923. Like the grim reaper of the Egyptian Tarot,[25] Toomer's reaper carries a scythe to reap his harvest without the assistance of northern machine technology. Interestingly enough, "Harvest Song" is the seventeenth poem in *Cane*. The Death Card, also known as the Grim Reaper in the Tarot, is the seventeenth card in the Tarot deck. Its reverse face meaning is nothingness. As the Destruction Cycle continues, the images of this new kind of death, this rampant sickness, intensifies in "Bona and Paul."

In the Incursion Cycle the narrator begins and ends as a third-person omniscient narrator. In the Atrophy Cycle the narrator begins as an involved first-person narrator, then moves back into a third-person voice with accompanying male characters speaking for themselves. In "Avey" in the Destruction Cycle, the narrator returns to a first-person voice. In the remaining work in the Destruction Cycle, the writing has male characters who speak more directly for themselves. The reader understands who and what they are more directly from their own dialogue. As *Cane* shifts the setting to go farther north—to get further away from the South—this pattern of having a male character speak continues in "Bona and Paul." Founded by a French African, Chicago is the apex of the Great Migration out of the South. Paul has negated his racial and cultural identity by "passing" as a Euro-American man at a teacher's training institute in Chicago. Jack M. Christ outlines the names in "Bona and Paul" as metaphors for sterility, nothingness, and negativity or puns on historical figures.

> Art Carlstom, whose last name reduces to Scandinavian for "colorless man," represents art that is bloodless, effete, and artificial. His girlfriend Helen suggests the conventional, self-indulgent, sentimental heroine who might easily imagine herself as the fatal Helen of Troy. ... Although she is also spoiled and self-indulgent, Bona Hale's first name puns on the Latin word for "good," and her last name is a double pun on "healthy" and "hail," as in "Hail, Mary." ...
>
> And Paul Johnson's name conjures several more echoes. His last name foreshadows Father John and all that he represents in "Kabnis." His first name puns first on "pall," a dark mourning cloth, and thus suggests his impact on those around him.[26]

As Paul struggles to understand how people perceive him, a sudden realization—people staring at him dancing with a Euro-American woman—makes him stop and acknowledge his difference to himself. Paul is the first male narrator in *Cane* to do this. Awakening to his own universe, he rejects the need for artificial ignorance or innocence in acknowledging and accepting differences in others. As Paul attempts to bring Bona to similar conclusions about race and caste, using logic, he represents the African-American struggle with the dialectical legacy of southern gentility. The dialectic is that Bona, like southern Euro-Americans in particular and Euro-Americans in general in 1923, will either "hate or love a nigger" but not accept the difference of skin color.

Bona struggles to understand the relationship between her feelings for Paul and her anxieties about how people perceive him. She thinks that "he is a harvest moon. He is an autumn leaf. He is a nigger," she finally admits to herself. Bona's designation of Paul as a nigger—not a Negro—who is passing is an important cue to her perception of him as an inferior being. However, she senses the dichotomy in this attitude because Paul proves that he is clearly her physical and intellectual match and she resents being proven wrong and being viewed critically by African-Americans.

Paul only manages to awaken himself enough to see the importance of his dark skin and his connection to the obviously African-American doorman, whose hand he goes to shake. He is unable to awaken Bona. When Paul returns to the place where he left her standing momentarily, she is gone. He is left to ponder the meaning of her disappearance, as well as to decide on a course of action appropriate for his new level of awareness. Since Paul is another mask of perceiving, creating the "I" voice of the male narrator throughout *Cane,* the new awareness drives him back to the South to resolve the dilemma within himself once and for all. The end of the story continues the Destruction Cycle and ends the northern urban section of *Cane.*

Paul, reappearing as Ralph Kabnis, represents "the neuroticized Black consciousness of the north, in quest of its uprooted spiritual and racial identity by means of a return to the moon-filled Southland of moon children." [27] Kabnis suffers from internal as well as external fragmentation, and he is genuinely baffled by the horrific chaos around him. He does not understand the way the world around him (in Georgia, 1923) works. His understanding of what he is and how he is supposed to exist in the American environment, North or South, indicates a "necessary schizophrenia" that is destroying him by rendering him dysfunctional. He has to find a way to heal himself or face death or insanity.

Throughout *Cane,* but especially in "Bona and Paul" and "Kabnis," Toomer uses sex to present each character's view of his or her own humanity. Allowing African-American characters to have and discuss sex was a critical point of development in African-American writing. Ralph Kabnis's superficial, indolent view of sex reveals the level at which he functions on other personal matters. Kabnis fails to resolve the personal matter of living in America as an African-American. Therefore, it is at the personal level that we meet him, paranoid, walking in a "dreamworld" that only he can see.

> His art is unable to tame Negro life, to transcend and so to affirm its vitality.

Kabnis also feels uneasy about being a Negro and a writer, which is miscegenation between earth and God.

Kabnis tries to integrate the spiritual and racial roots of the disparate parts of him which represent master and slave in America. He finds it difficult to do because he must learn to love himself and learn to love the African-American people who make up the African slave part of his heritage. That emotion, along with faith in his worth as an individual, is necessary for his rebirth at the end of *Cane.* "Toomer reaches the conclusion that love is the answer in the form of the charitable merciful figure of Carrie Kate, who attends the blind Father John with the understanding of one who has seen." [28] Thus, while "Kabnis" begins by continuing the Destruction Cycle, it ends by signaling the beginning of the Rejuvenation Cycle. Kabnis is the gold-glowing child—the sun (God incarnate) that, in finding the strength to go up the stairs to face reality, "steps into the sky and sends a birth-song slanting down gray dust streets and sleepy windows of the Southern town" to which he has returned. *Cane* has brought us full circle in the Great Migration through the four cycles developing the consciousness of the narrating voice. What remains is for the reader to understand the root images of *Cane,* as an extension of blues artistry— the ability to use place to define personhood—and to link that analysis to the Vertical Technique dynamics.

CHAPTER 3
The Vertical Technique—
Sociological and
Historical Groundings

I have uncovered no evidence that critics have identified a formal heuristic like the Vertical Technique to analyze any black literary work. Ordering the characterizations and plot of *Cane* through the Vertical Technique explains the novel's sequences as an attempt to compare the lives of African-Americans who live in the South and whose descendants migrated to the North or were delivered there, to look for the American Dream.

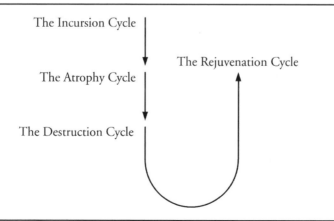

The Incursion Cycle

The Rejuvenation Cycle

The Atrophy Cycle

The Destruction Cycle

▶ Figure 3.1 Diagram of the Vertical Technique

The Vertical Technique's instructional value lies in its depiction of *Cane* as a unified work. The student cannot come to grips with the various themes unless he or she can decipher how the various parts of the book are related to one another; and clearly, even the critical reviewers of the book saw little continuity. The Vertical Technique organizes the novel's sequences to reveal the frustrated evolution of the mulatto male narrator's environment and the people in *Cane*'s southern and northern environments. It segments the action in *Cane* into four cycles that show the relationship between the shared problems and pain of the characters, as victims of the American racial dilemma. The adjective *vertical* is used here to illustrate the male narrator's tendency toward negative evolution in his racial identity. The stages that he goes through reflect a downward or negative motion that climaxes in two murders.

The Vertical Technique is an analytical device that uses elements of the African and African-American historic situation to present the world-view of Africana people—the worldview Toomer entered into during his Georgia residence and at other periods. Since an ethnic ontology is an inherent part of the literary imagery of *Cane,* the Vertical Technique provides a balanced and appropriate tool for explicating *Cane*'s structure and theme. The truth that is revealed is a part of the world constructed primarily by two opposing forces: Black Nationalism and White Racism.

Within this formula Black Nationalism does not and cannot equal White Racism but rather acts as a defensive response to it. As a concept, Black Nationalism unites Africana people throughout the world on the basis of racial heritage. In the Americas, however, Africana people represent combinations with many ethnic minorities, and it is not always easy for them to find cohesive elements with which to forge a coalition. Indeed, cultural dispersion often leads people of African descent to miss the characteristics and the conditions that they do share. The one outstanding characteristic that they share worldwide is social, economic, and political oppression by Europeans and European-Americans. Therefore, it is on this point that Black Nationalism is able to bring them together. The concept of Black Nationalism, as it has been used in the Americas, is closely related to the concept of Negritude and Pan-Africanism as ideological principles that forward African-American economic and social freedom. As P. Chike Onwauchi explains:

> Negritude is saying that the African world is the world of man ... characterized by spiritual and economic communalism, collective human consciousness and humanistic-orientated development. ...

> The essence of Negritude, must be articulated in Afro-centrism, the perspective in which the black man is objectively translated in his true essence of being as a

WHOLE-MAN and not as a pathological adjunct on the invisible man in the white-dominated world. The ideology of Negritude can best be realized if we can focus on what black people have in common all over the world (that is the white problem) rather than focus on what divides black people as human beings.[1]

Nationalism and racism are a result of a kind of extreme race consciousness that serves a defensive function.[2] While both forces act to protect each group's interest, neither force is able to build a country composed of many groups. Part of Toomer's argument for a more equitable America lies in his systematic deconstruction of classical images out of the African-American experience, as it portrays the American experience in *Cane*.

Through the Vertical Technique, this study interprets the history of class and race oppression and sexism in *Cane* that is subtlety represented by symbol and myth, though the two lynchings (one male and one female) are very graphically portrayed. The Vertical Technique suggests that there are implicit and implied relationships between African people in Africa and Africana people throughout the world as a result of the holocaust of the Atlantic Slave Trade. These relationships extend through the long historical process that established a triangular trade link between Europe, America, and Africa beginning in the fifteenth century.[3] The Atlantic Slave Trade facilitated the abduction of millions of Africans to establish an economic system that is the foundation of modern capitalism in Europe and America.[4]

Initially, both Africa and America were peripheral to the central power, mercantilist Europe. As the sources of free labor and raw materials, they provided "the setting" and "the actors" for European countries to compete in expansionist activities. However, the result has been that the important Africana communities (outside of the African continent) emerged in America and the Caribbean. "The impact of the Atlantic Slave Trade on the formation of primitive (financial) capital, that led to the Industrial Revolution in Europe and the New World, is well known; as are the disastrous consequences of this slave trade on African societies."[5]

The traditional American view of the impact of the Atlantic Slave Trade did not consider the extent to which the history and culture of African societies were altered by the loss of millions of its skilled artisans, philosophers, artists, and leaders. Only in modern times has the Atlantic Slave Trade been reexamined and analyzed from the point of view of the African, African-American, and Afro-West Indian. The work of Terry Alford in the book *Prince among Slaves,* Joseph Harris in the article "The Kingdom of Futa Djalon," Winston McGowon in the article "The Relations between the Europeans and Futa Djalon, 1794–1896," Walter Rodney in the book *Upper Guinea Coast 1545–1800*, and Ivan Mendez in the article "Resistance to Slavery in West Africa during the Eighteenth and Nineteenth Centuries" make it increasingly clear that the Africans who remained in Africa and the Africans who were taken to the Americas were subjected to identical forms of economic exploitation, identity crises, cultural manipulation, and psychological degradation. Moreover, because of these "shared" experiences, as well as their initial common culture, Africans and African-Americans face similar problems in transcending the cataclysmic effects of the Atlantic Slave Trade. These effects include problems related to miscegenation and political segregation. They share similar problems, too, in their attempts to evolve and develop independent postcolonial cultures.

The concepts of Black Nationalism, Negritude, and Pan-Africanism are political and philosophical responses to this complex dilemma. Nevertheless, they have not been the primary medium for solving these problems or for creating literary works that could help educate or orientate a new generation of Africana people around the world. It is at this junction that it becomes possible to discuss the relationship between the Harlem Renaissance and the Negritude Movement and what specific elements of the Vertical Technique merge their philosophies to clarify *Cane*.

The Vertical Technique is a tool that makes intelligible the African dispersion, as it is represented in the work of Africana writers. It transcends the traditional logic of Occidental languages and European history to describe the complexities of a human situation that is incredibly inhuman and chaotic.

In *Cahier d'un Retour au Pays Natal* published first in 1939, Negritude founding father Aimé Cesaire makes the connection between slavery and capitalism obvious. The Africans who built Virginia, Tennessee, Georgia, and Alabama inherited Jim Crow Law. Madagascaran poet Joseph-Casimir Rabearivelo, who changed his name to Jean-Joseph Rabearivelo in *Translations from the Night* written during the Harlem Renaissance in Madagascar and published after his 1937 suicide (translated into English in 1968 by John Reed and Clive Wake), structures the poetry of the same image more surrealistically, so that the effect of displaced or deranged naturalism leads the reader to understand that something is very wrong. Toomer replicates these literary strategies.

Cesaire asks,

"Who and what are we? Excellent Question!"[6]

Toomer in *Cane* asks this question over and over again in the challenge of the text's illogic as it describes the nature of behavior in a democratic society. Rabearivelo's clarity, without polemical language, is frighteningly haunting like Toomer's voice in *Cane*.

> This slave tricked out with beads of glass
> is as tough as Atlas
> and carries the seven heavens on his head.[7]

Aimé Césaire eloquently describes the dilemma of the educated Africana person who yearns to return to his native land to improve the fate of his people. It was this same aspiration (toward root vestiges of Africana culture) that inspired writers such as Langston Hughes, Zora Neale Hurston, Claude McKay, James Weldon Johnson, and others.

> I should come back to this land of mine
> and say to it: (Embrace me without
> fear ... If all I can do is speak, at least I
> shall speak for you).[8]

Cane would have the reader accept and speak for the American South (as a site of authentic Africana culture) with the hope that such recognition and reconciliation will help reduce the effect of the crimes birthed by the Atlantic Slave Trade.

ENGAGEMENT

CHAPTER 4
Using the Blues Motif to Analyze Cane

The Vertical Technique and the Blues Motif expand traditional notions of literary classification and broaden the boundaries of criticism and literary history to include works with roots deep in the oral and musical patterns of African-American life. Jason Berry makes a plea for such expansion in "Jazz Literature." He indicates that "*Cane* ... follows in the tradition of polyrhythmic music: part narrative and part verse. *Cane*'s beautiful, often haunting lyricism is something of an anomaly in the history of the [American] novel ..."[1] The Vertical Technique has evolved out of the need to explicate the lives of Africana people in Africana Literature. These people were living, struggling, and dying in reality and in literature under the rule of people with European personalities, attached to and centered by European culture. These two devices provide a literary macrostructure through which one can view *Cane* and make sense of its various stages. The illogic of *Cane* is the illogic of Africana existence within its own indigenous setting.

The Blues Motif, as a literary tool, augments the Vertical Technique's macrostructural view at the microstructural level by focusing on specific, individual images containing the dialectical symbolism. This symbolism contains both the sources of the stress and agony in *Cane,* as well as the cost of it having to be borne. The verbalization of this unbearable truth in blues imagery signifies African-Americans' ability to endow their lives with communicable significance and beauty.

In search of a definition of the blues, in *Listen to the Blues,*[2] Bruce Cook makes the analogy of the blues lyric (poem) to a couplet stretched

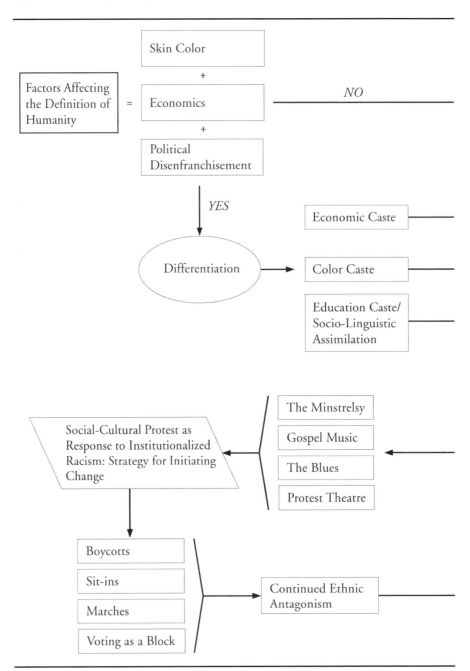

▶ **Figure 4.1 Diagram Tracing the Generation of the Blues Motif.** Designed by Chezia Thompson Cager. Typography and Imaging by Angelo Alcasabas.

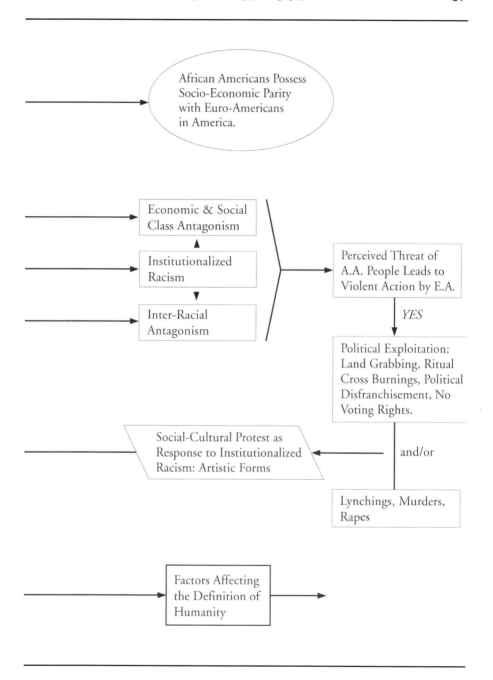

to three lines, allowing time for the blues musicians to invent the final line of the stanza. Each of the three lines consists of four bars, giving us the standard twelve-bar blues chorus. Yet it is more than a couplet stretched to three lines, simply by representing the first line before following with the second. Cook says the blues is deceptively simple by construction.

> Harmonically, blues was—at least in the beginning—a very simple form, but one that had a trick or two in store for the performer who thought he could pick it up just by reading the right notes ... the trick in blues harmony is in the so called "blue note." The third, fifth and seventh notes of the major scale are flatted, diminished to produce chords that can only truly come together in a quarter tone: horns and stringed instruments can "bend" into them; but a piano can only suggest it with a dissonant chord, for the true quarter tone lies, as they say, "between the keys." ... Some say these quarter tones were brought from Africa; they are the black contribution to Western harmony.
>
> And so if, in the blues scale, we drop certain tones from major to minor, the effect is basically a sad sound. And that, of course, is what the blues is all about: sadness, despondency.[3]

Cook goes on to discuss the significance of blue as a color correlated with depression and the devil in American English language and literature, including African-American novelist Walter Mosley's novel *Devil in a Blue Dress* and its association with altar construction (having four horns) in the Blue Lodge of the Prince Hall Masons.[4] Cook's point of view supports the argument for the subversion of the blues as an art form in mainstream culture over many years.

On the other hand, philosophically African-Americans (via the honored and esteemed legacy of the Prince Hall Masons) had a different view of blue as a color. Blue was holy as the color of the vault of heaven, which covers the entire planet. It is the symbol of universal friendship and benevolence within Africana communities. It is the color of the Madonna's clothes, depicted in portraits of Mary holding Jesus. To assign blue to something was to endow it with the power to nurture and to support survival. This study, in its translation of the blues from a musical art form into the blues as a literary motif, draws on the above Africana view of blue as a descriptor and a less-academic definition forged by bluesmen themselves. "The blues are the facts of life,"[5] says Willie Dixon, a major figure in the post–World War II blues tradition. He has been responsible for many of the hit recordings by blues giants such as Muddy Waters, Howling Wolf, Little Walter, Bo Diddley, Sonny Boy Williamson, Koko Taylor, and a host of others. He was a well-known recording and performing artist in his own right. In a 1980 discussion with Delta Blues

Festival organizers, Mississippi visual artist and blues musician James "Son Ford" Thomas expands Dixon's statement to indicate creating the blues is an act of power, a struggle to realize one's humanity in an impossible situation.

Academic research (which values proof of individual ownership as evidence of the rights to property within a capitalistic matrix) puts the birth of the blues at 1912, when the first songs were copyrighted[6] in St. Louis, Missouri. W. C. Handy's 1914 "St. Louis Blues" has been described as the most influential American song ever written because of its frequent international air play. Handy's autobiography *Father of the Blues* uses his life as a bluesician extraordinaire to discuss the condition of African-Americans at the beginning of the century and how that condition is intimately connected to American capitalism and the birth of the blues as an art form.

One can argue that the blues actually came into being as a distinct art form in 1897, with the performance of "Buddy Bolden Blues" in New Orleans. This study supports Samuel B. Charters's position in *The Bluesmen*[7] that designates the Mississippi Delta region as the cradle of the blues tradition in America long before the 1800s. W. C. Handy writes the blues after he works as a black minstrel and band leader in Mississippi from 1903 to 1905: living with the posted southern signs saying, "Nigger don't let the sun go down on you here," as a posted threat. In the Delta, the doctrine of separate and unequal existence posed a dilemma for the African-American men and women and poor Euro-American men and women that they often worked with and for farmers. Both groups saw themselves as completely human; but one group was denied the right of being human under the law. Handy's lyrics, "I hate to see de eve'nin' sun go down" rival Toomer's sense of the paradox of the beauty and the danger surrounding Karintha in "Her skin is like dusk on the eastern horizon ... When the sun goes down." The business of "acting out" one's manhood is a preoccupation with the rival characters in *Cane* and still poses a strategic problem related to the number of murders and violent acts for African-Americans in contemporary America.

As an analytical tool the Blues Motif derives its structure and purpose from the blues as a musical form. Created as a form of folk music by the African in America, the blues grew out of work songs, field hollers, traveling songs, story songs about dancing, gambling, drinking, and taking drugs. The blues grew out of songs about the rural experience, the urban experience, going to and being in jail, surviving natural disasters, and the phenomenon of death. In other words, the blues chronicles the African-American experience with an honesty and artistry that evolved out of the peculiar position in which the African found himself in the New World. Leonard Goines notes in "The Blues as Black Therapy" that because of the restrictions placed on African-American slaves after the slave revolts in Hispaniola (1522), Panama (1531), Cuba (1533), and Mexico (1537), their freedom of expression became even more limited than it had been. Their expression had to be communal, and it could not be reminiscent of the vibrant, throbbing drumming that had become associated with the African tradition and slave revolt communication. Instead, "a majority of the blues deals with situations and/or problems about which the Black man feels a sense of helplessness and/or confusion: those situations in which he questions his ability to arrive at a resolution to the problems involved."[8] Goines insists that the blues lyrics, written mainly by men (in the beginning), were designed to ask questions so that they could see and understand the nature of their problem—with the understanding that if they could just grasp the enormity of the situation they could create a solution to any related problems.

Black women blues singers take the blues form one step further. They make it a record of their experience as dispossessed humans at the bottom of a caste system from which there is no escape. Daphne Duval Harrison in "The Blues from the Black Woman's Perspective" cites from her research that the themes of women's blues lyrics are generally the same as those of men: They write about love, sex, death, frustration, infidelity, alienation, and freedom. However, Harrison points out, "The point of departure seems to be how women responded to these concerns and the frequency with which generic themes were dealt with."[9] Black women's blues tends to be more serious. It does not joke or kid about loss or oppression, and it expresses emotional devastation more frequently in the form of negative resolutions, nightmares, suicidal attempts, bad health, hallucinations, and violence. The women lyricists used the form to record their anguish, to exorcise their spirit, so that they could go on with life. Their language usage reflects the way Jean-Joseph Rabearivelo handled language in poetry in Madagascar early in the 1900s. He used it to fight the internal depression and utter despair at the futility of life in a colonial or neocolonial society that measures humanity and assigns economic and political opportunities on the basis of skin color.

The use of formal literary devices, such as figurative language, similes, metaphors, personification, and so forth, to portray "the historical destruction" of the African cultural context results in a poetic blues. As Stephen E. Henderson documents in his analysis in "Blues Poetry and Poetry of the Blues Aesthetic: A Study of Craft and Tradition,"[10] the blues poem is configured to be a fragment that resonates a more structural unifying aesthetic in remembering its musical tonal language ancestral past. In *Cane* Toomer uses the Blues Motif to create striking and impressive imagery as he reveals the remarkable range of African-American artistic folk expression. It is important to emphasize that the catharsis that appears in the dialectical images of *Cane* occurs at two levels: a personal or realistic level that challenges the day-to-day existence of the writer, and a creative or abstract level that utilizes language to make some sense of the contradictory elements shaping Toomer's life.

Discussing stellar Mississippi novelist Richard Wright, *Invisible Man*'s author Ralph Ellison says, "The blues is an impulse to keep the painful details and episodes of a brutal experience alive in one's aching consciousness, to finger its jagged grain and to transcend it, not by the consolation of philosophy but by squeezing from it a near-tragic, near-comic lyricism. As a form, the blues is an autobiographical chronicle of personal catastrophe expressed lyrically."[11] Gene Bluestein extends this definition in "The Blues as a Literary Theme": "We can see how far this is from earlier conceptions of Negro music as an expression of hopelessness and chaos. What emerges is an artistic form that makes possible the catharsis we usually associate with tragedy ... the blues does not skirt the painful facts of human experience, but works through them to an artistic transcendence."[12]

Toomer's method of presenting protest themes in *Cane* through the lives of women is a part of the legacy of the blues tradition in the twentieth century. Stanley Crouch's blues poem "Howling Wolf: A Blues Lesson Book" (on Flying Dutchman album "Ain't No Ambulances for No Nigguhs Tonight") focuses the energy of the blues lyric on a woman's power to redeem a man through the process of coitus. The poem seeks to preserve the essence of a fleeting aspect of African-American culture in a world preparing to take its technological revolution to the stars to escape a nuclear holocaust. If the reader takes either Toomer's disposition in *Cane* or Crouch's poem in consideration, he has to believe that a major thrust of the blues is the salvation of man in the body and love of woman.

The blues, with which Paul and Kabnis struggle, is only vaguely present in the male characters with names that come before them in *Cane*. However, in the descriptions and dialogue of the women, one finds the Blues Motif most prominent. Alice Walker chronicles the importance of seeing the lives of *Cane*'s women in the proper perspective in her book *In Search of Our Mothers' Gardens: Womanist Prose*.

> When the poet Jean Toomer walked through the South in the early twenties, he discovered a curious thing: black women whose spirituality was so intense, so deep, so unconscious, that they were themselves unaware of the richness they

held. They stumbled blinded through their lives: creatures so abused and muti-lated in body, so dimmed and confused by pain, that they considered them-selves unworthy even of hope. In the selfless abstractions their bodies became to the men who used them, they became more than "sexual objects," more even than mere women: they became "Saints." Instead of being perceived as whole persons, their bodies became shrines: what was thought to be their minds became temples suitable for worship. These crazy Saints stared out at the world, wildly, like lunatics—or quietly, like suicides; and the "God" that was in their gaze was as mute as a great stone.

For these grandmothers and mothers of ours were not Saints, but Artists; driven to a numb and bleeding madness by the springs of creativity in them for which there was no release. They were Creators, who lived lives of spiritual waste, because they were so rich in spirituality—which is the basis of Art—that the strain of enduring their unused unwanted talent drove them insane.

What did it mean for a black woman to be an artist in our grandmothers' time? In our great-grandmothers' day? It is a question with an answer cruel enough to stop the blood.[13]

Cane inadvertently answers Walker's question, while posing serious social and political questions of its own. If the Vertical Technique reveals the ravages of American racism and class oppression and sexism at a macroscopic level in *Cane,* the Blues Motif augments that structure by revealing the ravages of all of the same things at the systemic microscopic level of the individual. It allows the reader to examine specific images in *Cane* and see the dialectical symbolism as an artistic representation of a painful revealed truth. The art of the blues never reflects a state of chronic melancholia. Rather, it records a mood of profound, intimate dis-orientation. Toomer uses this device in *Cane* to signify a character's abil-ity to endow his or her life's incidents with communicable significance. That significance is that *Cane*'s themes and personalities are "oracular." Benjamin F. McKeever stresses the importance of the adjective *oracular* in *Cane.*

To be oracular is to be prophetic, for an oracle is not simply a messenger but a harbinger. The oracle vouchsafes a prediction which is not merely a forecast but a talisman, a way of dealing with the fate foreseen. *Cane* is oracular, document-ing as it does a Southern milieu, naming a certain malaise; but proffering only the alembic of Experience coupled with the vision of the artist."[14]

The women in *Cane* are apprentices in suffering. As Alice Walker indi-cates, the reader sees them trapped, without hope of being reprieved in the twilight of the post-Reconstruction period that Toomer's grandfather helped shape as acting governor of Louisiana.

INCURSION CYCLE

The Attack on the Reality of Southern Rural Life in the African-American Community

Place: The South, the Countryside in Georgia in 1923

Karintha is the first of those apprentices in *Cane*. For her, Toomer utilizes the repetitive, syncopated structure of the blues refrain.

> Her skin is like dusk on the eastern horizon
> O can't you see it, O can't you see it
> Her skin is like dusk on the eastern horizon
> ... When the sun goes down.

The 1980 *Oxford American Dictionary* defined dusk as "the darker stage of twilight." Dusky means shadowy, dim, dark, colored. Karintha is a comely beauty, like Solomon's biblical Sheba. She has "color" and is beautiful in an era that promoted the image of the "voluntary" Negro as the standard of beauty for all African-Americans. Karintha is a self-contained, vibrant spirit that seeks only to be itself. However, she is heir to the legacy of beautiful African-American women as concubines in the South. Thus, she is molded to function as a concubine. The succinct blues images show her in irresolvable, dialectical situations. "Men had always wanted her, this Karintha, even as a child." The lust of grown men for a child, an act that does not fit into the cultural matrix of African tradition, is unthinkable in moral terms, and yet, Karintha grows up surrounded by this hunger for her body.

There are other images. "Karintha is a woman. She who carries beauty, perfect as dusk when the sun goes down. She has been married many times." Karintha's perfect beauty doesn't help her to be any happier than an ugly African-American woman. They share the same fate in the same time and place. Karintha, in fact, appears to be less happy, since she either keeps losing or changing husbands.

> Old men remind her that a few years back they rode her hobby horse upon their knees. Karintha smiles and indulges them when she is in the mood for it. She has contempt for them.

Karintha knows the truth of the old men's lust for her even as a child. As a woman, she now knows how that lust warped her life. She makes the men pay. "They all want to bring her money." Karintha will not birth a life as a gift for any of them. "But Karintha is a woman, and she has had a child. A child fell out of her womb onto a bed of pine needles in the forest." Karintha aborts and burns the child she has conceived and delivered as a sexual object. Objects don't have babies, and the earth is cool or cold at dusk because there is little sun to warm it. Although infanticide was more acceptable during slavery (as a form of revolt), by 1923 the African tradition of valuing children (above all other things or entities in the environment) had been reinstituted with the promise of full citizenship as an American. Though then, as now, there could have been profound personal reasons to perform abortion or infanticide, generally there should not have been any political reasons to deny an African-American child life in the postbellum period. Karintha's ability to kill her child is proof that she is "cold." Her skin, the encasement of her soul, the embodiment of all of her senses, is like dusk, "When the sun goes down. Goes down ..."

In "Becky" the Blues Motif is presented as a gospel song. The religious overtones of the character Becky's supplication do not distract the reader from seeing that the blues images function in the same way. "Becky was the white woman who had two Negro sons." As the image of grown men having sex with a girl child is intolerable, so is the image of a "white woman" in 1923 willingly having sex with an African-American male. The social obscenities within the culture in 1923 seem to distort reality. Toomer punctuates the narrative in "Becky" with Becky's voice as if he is delivering a sermon, a blues sermon about a woman who was a living-dead.

> "The pines whisper to Jesus ... O fly away Jesus ... O thank y Jesus ... O pines, whisper to Jesus: tell Him to come and press sweet Jesus-lips against their lips and eyes ... O pines, whisper to Jesus ... O pines whisper to Jesus ... Pines shout to Jesus!"

These are the same pine trees that watched Karintha abort her child and burn it in pine needles, with no repercussions from the African-American or Euro-American community. However, in Becky's case both African-American and Euro-American communities judge her guilty of a heinous crime; though they support her through the twenty-year isolation, living on an "eye-shaped piece of sandy ground" islanded between the road and the railroad tracks. The man who fathered Becky's African-American sons is never discovered. He appears either to have worked within the community network to help her or to have abandoned her and the boys altogether. There is no way to know from Toomer's text. However, the reader does know that, either way, his life would have been forfeited had his identity been suspected or confirmed in a pre-blood-test, pre-DNA-test society. His blues of secrecy and Becky's blues of isolation are two mutual tragedies joined in the Incursion Cycle to warn the society that change is coming in the form of two young, angry African-American men.

As the image of child molestation and interracial sex is intolerable in 1923, so the sanctioned concept of beauty in the South does not allow a woman who is as strong as any man to be sensual, sexy, and coquettish. Carma, in overalls, is all of this and more. Carma's blues is sung by a girl, in the yard of a white-washed shack. Her blues song starts a dog in heat to howling at the moon: hence, the metaphor connecting howling, blues, moon, and wolf. (Howling Wolf was a famous blues singer.) It is a metaphor for Carma's soul, which is "weak and pitiable for so strong a woman." "Carma" begins and ends with a blues lyric.

> Wind in the cane. Come along
> Cane leaves swaying, rusty with talk,
> Scratching choruses above the guinea's squawk,
> Wind is in the cane. Come along.

The spirit is moving and it is time to return to the cane field. One may go there to hear the counsel of the talking cane leaves, which are older than man by rejuvenated generations on many continents; although more often than not people went to the cane field to work or to make love in privacy. Carma's fundamental nature comes from a primeval, agrarian origin. The cane field is her home, her substitute for the fertile, African forest that she left behind generations ago.

Carma's blues is that her tale, which is her life, is a crude melodrama. She is forced to act in the play without being able to revise the plot or modify the characterizations. Nevertheless, she knows, as the reader knows, that life is not a drama (even when it is dramatic) and that her dilemma is very real. If Karintha's blues dilemma lies in her struggle against being raised as a concubine and Becky's blues dilemma lies in the non-Europeanness of her children, then Carma's blues dilemma juxtaposes the strength of her body impulses and desires against the weakness of her mind and will.

ATROPHY CYCLE

The Continued Withering Away of Southern Rural Culture and Personality in the African-American Community

Place: Still the South, the Countryside in Georgia in 1923

In a completely different vein, Fern's blues dilemma lies in the differentiation of her body as her own, from her soul as God's property. Despite her known sexual activity, Fern is declared a virgin because men saw her as a being above them. Fern's dilemma is that she is torn between emotions that push her toward both coitus and cosmic consciousness. Men idolize her body and fear her soul. An African-American woman draws Fern's blues on the courthouse wall in the form of the mother of Christ. Fern's eyes can hold God and the countryside simultaneously: But how can she be African-Jewish in America? Arnold Rhodes in *The Mighty Acts of God* notes:

> Earlier we saw that there was a Hebrew people but no Hebrew race. It is equally true that those who participated in the Exodus were not confined to the Children of Jacob. "A mixed multitude also went up with them" (compare Num.11:4). No doubt this mixed multitude included quite a variety. It is probable that some of them were other groups of Habiru. ...
>
> Where did the Hebrew come from? According to ancient records there was a group of people known as the Habiru. It seems that these people were not a particular racial or national group but were nomadic wanderers throughout the Near East. They cannot be identified with the Hebrews in a simple equation, but it is possible that the Hebrews were a specific group within the larger group of nomads.[15]

Toomer's text suggests Fern's ancient birthright has overtaken her in modern times; as her name suggests a contemporary mixed heritage probably not unlike her ancient mixed heritage.

Her interior world is staggering. Her body is tortured with the strain. She tries to sing, but her voice is broken, a child's voice or an old man's voice. She has no mechanism of expression. Fern must hold the souls of the men (who bring her their bodies), God's presence, and the conditions of life for African-American people (sanctioned by the courthouse) in her cream-colored solitary consciousness. Neither Gentile nor Jew but both, Fernie Mae Rosen holds all pain for both groups of people, as the biblical Mary bore the pain of the world as the mother of God incarnate. Understandably, Fern sits mesmerized at the beginning and the end of the story. "Nothing ever came to Fern." Fern's blues dilemma is the sacrifice of her self and sexuality to an idea of sacredness that she can hold in reserve for an entire community, that in segregation acts as if nothing is sacred.

Place: Still the South but Now Moved to a Small Town's Main Street in Georgia, 1923

"Nothing ever came to Fern." And nothing comes to Esther, as she sits trapped in a caste system that is determined by skin color. Esther looks like a Euro-American child and her father is the richest colored man in town. That means she is somehow better than other African-American people but not good enough to be accepted by mainstream American society. Esther's blues dilemma lies in her color and her caste situation among oppressed people.

She is a pariah whose color caste warps her view of potential sexual and marriage mates. She dreams of having sex with Barlo, a man to whom she has never spoken and with whom she does not have a relationship. She progresses in the story from being a child to being an unmarried virgin, whose bourgeois status requires that she remain a virgin until a worthy suitor becomes her husband. As an economic and social dependent in her father's household, she is not free to make such choices about her body and her life in 1923. Esther's blues dilemma is the daily torture of living a somnambulistic life, with no expressive outlet and no hope for escape in her lifetime.

DESTRUCTION CYCLE

The Destruction of Rural African-Americans and the Annihilation of the Illusion of Civilized Behavior in the Pastoral South

Place: Still the South but Now on a Small Town's Main Street in Georgia, 1923

In an opposing mode, Louisa is a blues singer. "Louisa sang as she came over the crest of the hill from the white folks kitchen ... Her lips trembled. The slow rhythm of her song grew agitant and restless. The women sang lustily. Their songs were cotton wads to stop their ears ..." The three lines of their song are a part of the traditional twelve-bar framework of the blues as music.

> Red Nigger moon. Sinner!
> Blood-burning moon. Sinner!
> Come out that factry door.

The planetary lights of the sun and the moon are mentioned as the products of God's creative work on day four of the biblical version of the creation of the world and man. The planets are described as lights that later become regarded as signs of God's observance or movement. The science of aeromancy,[16] divination of the future from the air and sky, evolved from this concept of cause and effect between luminous heavenly bodies. The biblical fact that they precede the creation of life on the planet and are part of the ritual maintenance of that life argues for their ability to see what is going to happen and thus offer the warning omens. Thus, card XVIII or The Moon in the major Arcana of the Tarot deck is always a reference to danger coming or overcome, enemies coming or overcome, false friends coming or overcome. Violent change is coming to Louisa this night and to the era that "Blood-Burning Moon" occupies. It is not such an absurd thought as we—sitting in the twentieth-first century on the brink of World War III—might think. Poet, mystic, occult scholar, political operative, and self-proclaimed prophet, the infamous Aleister Crowley thought that he saw change coming in 1919 and tried to warn people. That Toomer in his search for meaning would not have met Crowley, as he had met Gurjieff and Ouspensky, is implausible.

> Like the Old High Tory he is at heart, he romantically had thought that the war would be a clean wind to England. He thought that the war would be conducted, from the English side at least, in a gentlemanly fashion. A victory for England by these means, he thought, was certain, owing to moral superiority. But when Bottomley, Lord George, Northcliffe and Co. took command ["howling demagogues ... blackguarding" German literature, music and culture], Crowley came to the conclusion that the ideals of England as thus formulated, ought not to triumph. In high dudgeon he traveled to America. ...
>
> During his five years in America, he seems to have worked out a little more fully the ethical implications of such a religion ["Qabalistic"(sic) knowledge applied]; though in this respect also his activity was not so much a new departure as an intensification of earlier thinking on the subject. When he came back to Europe in 1919 and lived in a villa ... he seriously believed that the World War had signalised (sic) the breakdown of Christian civilisation (sic) and that his was the tremendously responsible part of teaching an ethical code of the new Aeon.[17]

Toomer's fiery red moon was a warning, bearing an uncanny resemblance to the apocalyptic blues lyrics of "Sinnerman, Where You Gon Run To."

> Oh, Sinnerman, where you gon run to ...
> the Lawd said, "Go to the Devil!" ...
> So I ran to the Devil, he was waiting ...[18]

In response to the music in Louisa's world, the dogs start howling again, and the reader learns that Louisa's blues dilemma comes in the irresolvable competition of an African-American man and a Euro-American man for her affection. She knows that she must choose. The laws of the South tell her that she must choose. The laws of the South tell her that she must. Nevertheless, she refuses to announce a choice and loses both men to needless deaths. The final image of African-American suitor, Tom Burwell, resembles the man in the famous Billie Holiday blues song "Strange Fruit."

> Blood on the leaves
> And blood at the roots
> Black body swinging in the southern breeze[19]

Louisa, helpless in her emotional disorientation, sings to the moon and the two dead men. It is a blues song about "niggers" and the moon, blood and sinning, and a fact'ry door that opened to death and never closed again.

"Rural Blues from the Delta"[20] by bluesicians[21] Mississippi John Hurt, Sam Chatmon, Furry Lewis, Skip James, James "Son" Thomas, Betty Mae Fikes, Alberta Hunter, and numerous other artists is the mother of Urban Blues as sung by B. B. King, Lightning Hopkins, John Lee Hooker, Koko Taylor, Sylvia Embry, Johnny Shines, Sippie Wallace, Billie Holiday, and others. As the Great Rural Migration moved to the cities in the South and then on to the North, so did the musical art of the blues. Toomer continues looking at the lives of women in the northern cycle (which is also the Destruction Cycle) of *Cane* in "Avey."

Place: The North, Seventh Street, Washington, D.C., 1923

"Avey's mother ont her ..." is almost untranslatable. One possible interpretation is Avey's mother wasn't her mother. Hence, Avey is an orphan. Her blues dilemma is that she carries her indifference as a shield against the terror of being alone, unclaimed, unpropertied, and unmarried in an age when a woman's whole existence is organized around such matters. Avey seems to be apart, separate from people in her environment; she has separated access to her body from access to her soul.

She is educated but will not pursue the dreams of middle-class professionals. Perhaps those dreams are too limited for her. Perhaps they are too foreign to her nature, which combines the physical and spiritual attributes of the women who came earlier in *Cane*. Avey will not occupy "a woman's place" in society; so she chooses to occupy no position at all. Twice orphaned, by the end of "Avey" she appears to be a well-dressed Washington, D.C., courtesan. The narrator thinks the valley train engine whistle gasps and sobs as "crude music from the soul of Avey." It is the blues song of the modern woman in a modern age who must find a viable economic path to walk to the future.

What the reader can find amazing about Avey is that without exerting any energy she is able to maintain control of herself as she makes choices about her life and creates the illusion of having control in her environment. She bears an uncanny resemblance to the age-old heroine "See-Line Woman," who in oral folklore is reputed to be the transplanted Yoruba saint of love, coquetry, fresh river water, and life as the essence of femininity. Her name in Nigeria is Oshun of the inland waters and Yemanya, mother of the sea. In Haiti her name is Erzulie, Lady of the Lake, and as mistress of love, she has also been given the power to harness hate to wage war when justified. These orishas or loas are more cultural constructs—instead of worshiped deities—by a people who have always believed that there is only one Creator God.

> Black dress on for a thousand dollars
> She wail and she moan
> See-Line Woman.[22]

This study sees Avey and See-Line Woman as examples of women possessed by the saint's spirit. Ezulie in Haiti is both elemental and human. Avey is passive but actively controls her relationships. She is seductive but does not entice men into a passionate embrace. The men, of their own accord, want more than her body. They want her to acknowledge them and their power. She is in the world but appears not to be a part of the world. Men appear to know very little about her. What they are sure of is that she moves them. "The girls up that way, at least the ones I knew, haven't got the stuff: they don't know how to love. Giving themselves completely was tame besides just holding Avey's hand."

For any poor, nonwhite, or culturally alienated person, living in America is an art form—that is, a creative production. Toomer explores this art form in the Destruction Cycle through Dorris's, Muriel's, and Bona's "man-trouble" blues dilemmas. In all three cases, the men involved are unable to love because they need more than a physical union. Each man has superficially categorized each woman, assigning her limitations that reflect his own neuroses. In "Theater," Dorris dances to tempt a lover. Her blues is the glorious song that is the muscles of her limbs. "And her singing is of cane-brake loves and mangrove feastings." The text tells us Dorris's sensuality and perception of self were born somewhere other than Washington, D.C., and she does not understand the caste system that controls propriety.

Dorris is an artist, and she uses her art form to enrapture John. How successful she is in doing this she will never know. John separates his body from his mind and allows his mental state—not his physical body—to become enraptured. Hence, Dorris cannot see his genuine and natural response to her artistic gift. "John's melancholy is a deep thing that seals all sense but his eyes and makes him whole." He is beyond her reach in the theater of his mind.

Muriel in "Box Seat" works diligently at subverting her own sexual and social nature. She loves Dan, but neither she nor Dan is strong enough to bear the burden of being together in the "box seat" of life, where everyone can see them and criticize their every word and action. Dan tries to sing, but he cannot, without hurting himself. "Muriel's lips become the flesh-notes of a futile, plaintive longing." It is a blues song of a woman caught between insanity and the trauma of having the comfort and company of the man that she loves. Dan discovers the formula that will free them. "Me horizontally above her. Action: perfect strokes downward oblique. Hence, man dominates because of limitation. Or so it shall be until women learn their stuff." In the end neither Muriel nor Dan actualizes their potential as humans in a love relationship. Muriel does not learn "her stuff" and Dan cannot teach her; they are thus both frustrated and lost.

Place: Chicago, Illinois, Segregated College Campus, 1923

The same end meets Bona and Paul. However, in this instance Paul is able to make the intellectual leap to understand the nature of Bona's passion. He discovers that mental concepts rule her in the same way that they rule John in "Theater." In both stories, John and Bona's mental concepts prevent them from loving and giving themselves in love to a person of their choice. Like Bob Stone in "Blood-Burning Moon," Bona faces her own earlier admission that she is attracted to Paul because she suspects that he is a "nigger." Bona's blues dilemma comes in the answer to the question she poses for herself, as she admits that she is interested in Paul. "Her answer is a crash of jazz from the plant-hidden orchestra. Crimson Gardens is a body whose blood flows to a clot upon the dance floor."

Paul is left alone in his passion but he understands the social and political context of the difference between his choice and Bona's, which is why his speech to the African-American doorman (who did not identify him as African-American in a "white only" establishment) is important. These three sets of would-be lovers in "Theatre," "Box Seat," and "Bona and Paul" cannot have constructive, fulfilling relationships because their neuroses (which have been shaped by their middle-class values) keep them apart and fragmented. Everyone but Paul is elementally destroyed as an actualized human being. Paul survives because he figures out the game of the "black" presence in America.

REJUVENATION CYCLE

The Rebirth of Something or Someone
or the Promise of Rebirth of Something or Someone

Place: The South, Small Town in Georgia, 1923

The most obvious Blues Motif occurs in "Kabnis." In it, the narrator observer, or the "I" voice of "Fern" and "Avey," rehearses the fate of a dream deferred. Benjamin F. McKeever in "*Cane* as Blues" describes the narrator's state as "an inanimate idea held by a weakling idealist, trapped in Hamletesque stasis." What Kabnis has in common with the women of *Cane* is the necessity of finding an artistic vehicle to express his alien- ation in the South. He does not want to be earth's child, who is southern and African-American. Neither does he want God, a "profligate, red-nosed man about town," for a father. He prefers being a bastard son, like Becky's two sons. "A bastard son has a right to curse his maker." Kabnis feels this loneliness, an awful, intangible oppression that could drive a man insane. He thinks of himself as "an atom of dust in agony on a hillside." These are all metaphors representing the Blues Motif.

In a pun on the blues aesthetic, Kabnis insists that his ancestors were southern "blue-bloods." Moments later he realizes, "Ain't much difference between blue and black," which McKeever says virtually equates being African-American with being destined to have the blues.

> Kabnis is born into the midst of an oppressed and persecuted people. He is one of them—a part of them and apart from them. He knows the unique experience of being the rejected and despised of men: sometimes one feels like a "mother- less child" and other times like a "manchild in the promised land" on the eve of the death of God, when only one's enemies have received the uncovenanted rev- elation of God's demise. ...
>
> For he knows and he feels that a man's life is not supposed to be a chronicle of personal catastrophe but rather a celebration: perhaps a poem, a song, a dance, a bacchanalia, a saturnalia, a romantic interlude before the final elegy. However, the difference between the possibility of black life and the reality of black life is the blues. Yet the blues idiom itself celebrates Life; it celebrates the will to endure and the necessity of survival, to "keep on keeping on."[23]

Ultimately, in the grave, ritualistic manner of "the laying on of hands," Carrie Kate helps to lift Kabnis from the state of being America's "hollow- sin." One way to see Toomer's consistent assignment of symbolic names is to interpret *Kab* as "hollow vessel" in Hebrew and *sin* as the inversion of *nis*. Thus, Kabnis's spiritual reckoning in her hands provides the uplifting hope anticipated in her exclamation, "Jesus, come," signaling the Vertical Technique's Rejuvenation Cycle. Kabnis tells her, "But twon't do t lift me bodily. You dont understand. But its th soul of me that needs th risin." As African-American women have over the centuries of their residence in the New World, Carrie Kate applies the needed balm to lift Kabnis. She uses her body and the love that ultimately defines woman as a cosmic entity able to endow the acts of blues people with power, through her blues art forms. Toomer's engagement with world religion had clearly taught him the power of the mind to establish physical states. The soul and the mind of African-Americans needed lifting to create a different kind of environment. While legislation was an important beginning to developing physical opportunity and equality for African-Americans, Toomer had higher ambitions for the heights of mental and physical health to which all Americans could rise through spiritual enlightenment. Kabnis is a glimpse of a weary man at the door of his soul's rising.

Toomer's love of wordplay or the art of naming suggests at least one more interpretation of Kabnis's name. If Kan and Cane as homonyms can be assigned the same meanings and added to Bis—or the name of Toomer's favorite uncle—it is possible to see Kabnis's meaning as the soul of Cane field/country/South and the soul of Bismark Robert Pinchback. Uncle Bis was Toomer's first live writer and model of conflict resolution. Here, as in other places, was the painted face of a member of his own family as an example of his own conflicting face of beauty staring into the mirror of the South.[24]

The Vertical Technique and the Blues Motif expand notions of literary classification and broaden the boundaries of criticism and literary history to more clearly explicate works with roots deep in the oral and musical patterns of African-American life. *Cane* mercilessly portrays the traumatic lives of Americans in Georgia, Washington, D.C., and Chicago in 1923. Toomer's work in *Cane* can be viewed as an examination of the stereotypes (see, for example, the female stereotypes in Figure 4.2) whose stories reflect traditional blues themes.

Toomer's investigation can also be seen as an examination of the relationship between economic status, sexual status, and the allocation of sociopolitical power as outlined in Figure 4.3.

Toomer's landscape includes farmers, southern belles, neoslave masters, professors, dancers, teachers, northern belles, journeymen, children, married women, single women, men-in-love, men-out-of-love, and spiritualists. Through the eyes of Ralph Kabnis, an African-American man who physically resembles a Euro-American man, *Cane* reviews Jean Toomer's growth as a human being traveling through the four cycles of the Vertical Technique.

Cane is also about love. It's not about invented clichés but the ultimate love/hate/love relationships between human beings in "a not-so-humane society." Lastly, *Cane* proves that, as Americans, we are fooling ourselves if we think the horrors of 1923 no longer exist. All of *Cane*'s problems (particularly the political and racial ones) remain with us in some form at the beginning of the twenty-first century. In the words of the early bluesicians, the only way out of this situation is "ta walk togetha chillen, n don't ya git weary."

Incursion Cycle:		
Karintha – As a Child	*The Fair Virgin*	Woman as Beauty Incarnate
Karintha – As a Woman	*The Siren*	Woman as Beauty Incarnate
Becky	*The Mother*	Woman as Scapegoat
Carma	*The Seductress*	Woman as Aggressive Sexual Being
Atrophy Cycle:		
Fern	*The Priestess*	Woman as the Vessel of God
Esther – As a Child	*The Prim Little Lady*	Woman as the Epitome of the Proper Social Values and Decorum
Esther – As a Youth	*The Tragic Mulatto*	Woman as the Victim of Color And Caste
Esther – As a Woman	*The Pariah*	Woman as a Being Estranged from her natural instincts and cosmic connection
Destruction Cycle:		
Louisa	*The Liberated Woman*	Woman as a Sexual Being
Avey	*The Pariah*	Woman as Self-determining Entity
Dorris	*The Temptress*	Woman as Artist
Mame	*The Gossip*	Woman as Artist
Muriel	*The Old Maid*	Woman as Integrated Middle-Class Professional
Mrs. Pribby	*Housewife/Matron*	Woman as Integrated Middle-Class Professional
Bona	*The Euro-American Temptress*	"White" Woman as the most sexually desirable and aggressive beings in an integrated Middle-Class society
Cora, Stella	*Sexual Objects*	Woman as an Object to be used for sexual release and gratification
Rejuvenation Cycle:		
Carrie Kate	*Housewife/The Fair Virgin; The Mother/The Priestess*	Woman as a manifestation of the Holy Spirit

▶ **Figure 4.2 Female Stereotypes in *Cane***

Economic Status	*Female Character and Associated Male Character*	Sexual Status
Incursion Cycle:		
Economically Dependent	*Karintha – The Child (Young African American boy)*	Unmarried Virgin
Economically Dependent	*Karintha – As a Woman (Many nameless men)*	Married, Divorced, Remarried many times
Economically Dependent	*Becky (Nameless man/men)*	Euro-American Unwed Mother
Farmer/Share Cropper	*Carma (Nameless man & husband, Bane)*	Married – Sexually Active
Atrophy Cycle:		
Economically Dependent	*Fern (Kabnis)*	Virgin by Proclamation – Unmarried – Sexually Active
Economically Dependent	*Esther – The Child (Barlo)*	Unmarried Virgin
Economically Dependent	*Esther – The Youth (Barlo)*	Unmarried Virgin
Economically Dependent: Works in Father's Store	*Esther – The Woman (Barlo)*	Unmarried Virgin
Destruction Cycle:		
Domestic	*Louisa (Tom Burwell & Bob Stone)*	Unmarried – Sexually Active with son of Euro-American Plantation Owner
Teacher/Paid Companion	*Avey (College Boys, Nameless Men, Kabnis)*	Unmarried – Sexually Active as she chooses – Orphan Woman
Dancer	*Dorris (John)*	Unmarried – Sexually Active in her imagination
Dancer	*Mame (John)*	Maybe Unmarried; Maybe sexually active
Home Owner/Boarding House Proprietor	*Mrs. Pribby (Dan Moore)*	Maybe Married in the past: Virginal demeanor
Middle-Class Professional Educator	*Muriel (Dan Moore)*	Unmarried – Virginal demeanor
Student Economically Dependent	*Bona (Paul=Kabnis)*	Unmarried – Sexually Active
Student Economically Dependent	*Helen (Art)*	Unmarried – Sexually Unknown
Economically Dependent Maybe Paid Companions Housewives	*Stella, Cora (Halsey, Lewis, Father John, Kabnis)*	Impression of being married or having been married – sexually active
Rejuvenation Cycle:		
Domestic	*Carries Kate (Kabnis)*	Unmarried – Virginal

▶ Figure 4.3 Economic Status of the Women in *Cane*

CHAPTER 5

Jean Toomer: The Relationship of Biographical Material to Understanding Cane

THE BLACK/WHITE DILEMMA:
THE LEGACY OF P. B. S. PINCHBACK

The proper historical orientation is very important to actualizing the instructional value of *Cane*. The era of legal segregation in America is as critical in forming Toomer's vision in *Cane* as are the facts of his biography. Both elements must be examined together to understand the male mulatto narrator's political and social commentary.

Eugene Pinchback Toomer, or Nathan Jean Toomer, was born in 1894 in Washington, D.C. He was the son of Nathan and Nina Toomer, who had married against the best wishes of Nina's father, P. B. S. Pinchback. These two men's lives had a profound effect on Jean Toomer's perception.

In "On Being American," Toomer states that P. B. S. Pinchback was born in Macon, Georgia. Pinchback's father was considered a white man of Scotch-Welsh-German stock. Pinchback's mother was said to have some "dark blood" that may have been of Negro, Indian, Spanish, or Moorish blood. When the family moved to a plantation in Mississippi, Pinchback ran away. Dissociated from his family, he got a job on a Mississippi steamboat, which he took to New Orleans. Toomer describes his grandfather's life in New Orleans as "precarious." With the advent of the Civil War, Pinchback organized a company for the Federal Army, but not before marrying Nina Hethorn. Toomer describes her lovingly:

Her picture ... shows a soft gentle face, sensitive and delicate, touched with a strain of timidity or meekness. It portrays a woman, essentially a wife and mother, the maker of a home, who will see the world only as it comes within her house or as it passes before her window at which she sits embroidering. And this in truth was my grandmother. Yet it was not all of her. For, as sometimes happens with apparently retiring and timid souls, somewhere in her there was a surprising courage and fortitude. She went with her husband to war-camp and there nursed her first child. She stood without flinching at Pinchback's side all through his stormy and dangerous political career. She saw the rise of the family and, out-living her husband and all but one of her children, she endured its rather tragic fall. She was the one person in my home who sustained her faith in me after I turned black sheep, who supported me through thick and thin. ... [1]

When the Civil War ended, Pinchback realized that African-American men had the heretofore unmentionable power to vote and elect their own officials. He was a man with political ambition but no significant constituency. Therefore, he chose to claim that he had "Negro blood" as a way of linking himself to the African-American pursuit of equal rights under the law. In this way Pinchback rose to power in the political arena in Louisiana. As the "Negroes' elected champion," he did very little for them except to set an example of how one lives well with the advantage of political status and money.

Toomer recounts two risks that Pinchback allegedly took in the name of the Freedman's cause. He also explains the motive behind his grandfather's actions.

I remember hearing of how on two occasions he risked his life in an effort to enact legislation favorable to the Negro. One was during the time when he was president of the state senate. Pinchback had been told that when a certain bill came up, his opponents would be armed and would try to stop him by force. Pinchback armed his supporters and had them stationed about the house. At his signal they were to fire. But they did not have to. With excitement running high, but with no violence, the day came and passed.

The other was the then famous railroad race with Warmouth. Warmouth was governor. Pinchback was Lieutenant-governor. Both of them were in New York at a banquet. Pinchback had an act he wished to put over; and he could do this if he could return to Louisiana before and without Warmouth, for then he would be acting-governor. When the banquet was at its height, Pinchback slipped out and boarded a train for New Orleans. At some little town down south this side of Louisiana, he was called from the train to receive a telegraph message in the station. Once he was in the room the door was shut and bolted—and there he was kept prisoner until Warmouth's special arrived. Warmouth, missing him and suspecting his design, had telegraphed ahead to have him detained. Having arrived on the spot, he had Pinchback released and told him that he was glad they had caught him just there. Otherwise, Pinchback would not have been among the living. Warmouth had sent orders that he was not to enter Louisiana alive.

But even these episodes, risky though they were, and done to a certain extent for the Negro, show the tactics, not of an idealist and liberator, but of a bold dramatic venturer.[2]

Pinchback became a well-known, picturesque figure in Louisiana during Reconstruction. From collector of the Port of New Orleans, to governor of Louisiana, to the US Senate, he wove a legacy of courageous, adventurous stories surrounded by racial ambiguity, until his local power ended with the demise of the carpetbaggers.

Pinchback believed in large families and ruled his household of three boys and a girl (Toomer's mother) as a patriarch. Nina was particularly victimized by his dual affectionate concern and disrespectful, domineering manner. The impact on her did not manifest itself forcibly until the family moved to Washington, D.C., in 1890.

Just out of finishing school, Nina Pinchback was an accomplished artist. She wrote poetry, sang, danced well, and developed the graces of a lady that made her her father's favorite. However, when Nina reached the age of marriage, her father was unwilling to let her go. She fought him unsuccessfully for the right to make decisions about her life until a fifty-two-year-old plantation heir, Nathan Toomer, appeared. Jean Toomer says the following about his father:

> At the age of 52, he was an upstanding figure, above medium height, broad shouldered, well-nourished, weighing around two hundred pounds. A flair for living invested his substantial physique with a romantic glamour. There was Dignity in the man, a certain richness and largeness, and charm. He had, in fact, quite a presence. And he had a way with people.
>
> ... The one time I saw him he had a brooding expression, a rather extraordinary expression. It came from deep within him and seemed to reach towards something far away. As I reflect on that expression now, a feeling comes to me that among his many puzzling features he may have had a streak of genius in him—a streak that never finding its proper occupation, disturbed his inner life and sometimes came to the surface in a mood of creative brooding.
>
> I search my memory of his picture. I search my memory of his face as I saw it in life. I search in vain for visual signs of the deceits and weaknesses that undoubtedly were there.[3]

Elsewhere Toomer adds:

> His father, a plantation owner, had left him some money, and Toomer lived as a gentleman of leisure with a taste for luxury and elegance. He was of English-Dutch-Spanish stock. I gather that he lived in the south as white man. Did he have Negro blood? It is possible. [4]

Nathan Toomer courted, wedded, and then deserted Nina Pinchback early in her pregnancy. It is with this history that she returned home from her rebellious love marriage to the unwavering tyranny of P. B. S. Pinchback. Eugene Pinchback Toomer (Jean Toomer) was born December 26, 1894, and raised in the household of his grandfather, who surprisingly took no active part in his upbringing. Toomer could hardly imagine that he would repeat his grandfather's opportunistic display of racial blend and then—like his grandfather—completely dissociate himself from being African-American.

In 1920, Toomer returned to Washington to take care of his dying grandparents and to make himself a writer. *Cane,* the South's swan song, is deeply intertwined with Toomer's grandfather's death. Pinchback died the day after Toomer finished the first draft of "Kabnis" in 1922. "That event preceded Toomer's emergence as an artist and it had, no doubt, psychic reverberations of great consequence."[5] Uncle Bismark, Toomer's favorite maternal uncle, died six months after *Cane* was published. His grandmother to whom *Cane* is dedicated died in September of 1928.

Toomer was converted to the religious and philosophical beliefs of Georges Gurdjieff in 1923, and after a summer study in 1924 (at the Gurdjieff Institute in Avon near Fontainebleau, France), Toomer returned to America as a disciple. Failing to recruit "New Negro" artists to his cause, he turned to the affluent and Euro-American artistic community. There he met with greater success, discovering, in Darwin Turner's words, "the primary purpose of literature is to teach." While teaching, writing, and searching for harmony and self-realization, Toomer met and married Euro-Americans Margery Latimer, who died in childbirth, and Margery Content, who remained with him until his death on March 30, 1967.

The ambiguity of Toomer's declaration of his own African-Americanness cannot be allowed to jeopardize the cultural and artistic value of *Cane. Cane*'s value as a literary work transcends any ambiguities about Toomer's life after 1923. As Taylor writes in "The Second Coming of Jean Toomer," "there are aspects of his work—his use of black folk idiom, his conception of Negritude and of the enigma of blackness—still not surpassed or exhausted by later black writers."[6]

GROWING UP WHITE IN AMERICA

When he was a child, Toomer's world was structured primarily by women. They included his mother, his grandmother, and the first love of his life, Dorothy.

But to return to Dorothy. One other thing she did was to stamp me with, to indelibly impress upon me her image. It was the image of a fair girl. My mother was dark. Already her picture, also fixed permanently, lay within me. And so the two, dark and fair, existed side by side, to govern my taste through-out life.

Blonde and brunette—two physical types, two kinds of women with whom a man can be in love. But in life nothing is only physical. There is also the symbolical. White and black. West and East. North and South. Light and Darkness. Day and Night. In general, the great contrasts. The pairs of opposites. And I, together with all other I's, am the reconciler.[7]

In this expository text, we have the first vision of the women of *Cane*. Light and dark, they reflect Toomer's complex view of women. Although Toomer insists that he was not raised to be a sexist, racist, or a religious fanatic,[8] the mode and method of his upbringing indicates that he was raised to have very definite prejudices in favor of being Euro-American, middle-class, and male. This bias affects the portraits in *Cane;* although Toomer does not say directly that being Euro-American, male, and middle-class is the best mode of being in America, he paints a dim picture of being African-American, economically disenfranchised, and female.

In "Earth-Being," Toomer says, "I was told there was God, but I was not told [that] I must love or fear Him." And in *Cane* we find God treated offhandedly, as a being who shares the blame for the lamentable situation in which men and women live in the South and the near-South. The concept of sin, along with the Judeo-Christian doctrine of Original Sin, was something that he had never heard of formally. Thus, if the reader accepts an analysis correlating Ralph Kabnis's behavior to the evolution of Jean Toomer, then Father John's declaration discerning the "sin of white folks" is a remarkable revelation about the nature of American society. Father John intimates that African-Americans and Euro-Americans base their lives on a lie that is dysfunctional for all Africana people anywhere. It is also a lie that thwarts the development of a productive existence for both African-Americans and Euro-Americans.

"Earth-Being" suggests that Toomer's lack of formal training in religion did not prohibit him from developing the "deep and powerful interior sense of religion," which Barlo, Dan Moore, and Kabnis exhibit in different ways. Many of the women (Carrie Kate, Fernie Mae Rosen, and the unnamed woman who draws the picture of the Black Madonna on the church wall) exhibit a similar depth of religious fervor. It is to this interior life that Toomer himself turned to garner the strength to overcome a severe illness. The "new affirmation" that emerged out of his battle to live was the turning point of his life.

I had been strong. Now I was weak. I was compelled to exert effort to get strong again. Life had taken away what it had given, and I was forced over years to obtain it by exertion. In fine, I was made to become energized in a new way, and struggle with myself. The Stream no longer completely carried me.

I had been active mainly externally. Now I could not be so. I gradually became active mainly interiorly [sic] and built up an inner world of my own in which intangible things were more real than tangibles.

... In short, the entire experience and its consequences were the shock and the circumstance which started my individualization.[9]

Soon after his illness, Toomer moved alternately to Brooklyn, New Rochelle, and New York, where he lived with his mother and stepfather between 1906 and 1909. Toomer's mother died on June 9, 1909, and he returned to live with his uncle on Florida Avenue in Washington, D.C. It was the first time he had experienced living in a "colored world."

Toomer chronicles the similarities between his Euro-American middle-class friends on Bacon Street and his African-American middle-class friends on Florida Avenue with the objectivity of a blind man. "Segregation, if known to them [his Florida Avenue friends] meant nothing. They were as youths of fifteen anywhere." It is inconceivable that his African-American friends could not have known of segregation or been affected by it. Segregation was the burning issue of the day that had suddenly forced the creation of the National Association for the Advancement of Colored People in May 1910. Because of segregation there were only one hundred colleges that African-Americans could attend in 1910, and this was the first year that those schools would accept women. Booker T. Washington and W. E. B. Du Bois carried their debate on the progress of the African-American to England, while Jack Johnson fought "The Great White Hope," Jim Jefferies, in the race fight of the century. That fight won him the title of heavyweight champion of the world and restored a measure of pride for African-Americans existing as displaced and denigrated warriors in America. The Jack Johnson win was a warning to America about the powerful sleeping giant it had temporally caged, but whose awakening could resurrect great power. The film of the Jack Johnson–Jim Jefferies championship fight created an interstate edict against fight films and may have convinced film producers to keep African-Americans out of movies.[10]

By 1910 residential segregation ordinances were enacted in Baltimore and already operational in Washington, D.C., which is why Toomer's two sets of friends were separate in his mind and in his life. Washington, D.C., had the largest African-American population in any US city in 1910. Its

African-American residents numbered 94,000 and represented every con-
ceivable human disposition and talent. With the decline of Negro min-
strelsy and the growth of the white hysteria accompanying the Great
Migration north, African-Americans were restricted to having theatrical
performances only in Harlem, New York. The US census identified
9,827,763 African-Americans in the United States that year.[11] Of that
underestimated number of people, 20% were singled out and formally
classified as people of "mixed blood," based on their color.

Segregation, in fact, was a way of life for African-Americans in
Washington in 1910 and continued to be well into the 1960s. Toomer's
color, however, allowed him to live as a non-Negro (not a Euro-American
person) and a voluntary Negro, who could un-enlist whenever he
wanted. This situation profoundly affected the way he perceived everything in American society. His position in the social order is the major reason much of *Cane* appears to be chronicled so objectively. Toomer was
recording the lives of exotics in much the same way Waldo Frank and
Sherwood Anderson were trying to record the lives of African-Americans.
It is probably more of an accident of superior craftsmanship, than intent
of purpose, that the reader is able to see the narrator's evaluation to race
consciousness and sexual awareness in *Cane*.

After he completed the eighth grade, Toomer entered N. Street High
School (later named Dunbar High School for Paul Laurence Dunbar),
where the mysteries of sex alternately confused and tortured him into
erratic, despondent behavior. He also began the ritual summer pilgrim-
ages to Harper's Ferry (the scene of John Brown's shoot-out with slave
owners over the issue of enfranchisement for African-Americans),
Arundel, and Annapolis that help us understand his love for Avey, who in
real life was probably Phyllis Terrell. Toomer arrived at a philosophical
racial stance during the period right after his high school graduation. (He
fulfilled all the requirements in three years.) This doctrine underscores
the hideousness of the crimes committed by and against the African-
Americans inhabiting *Cane*. Since Toomer's thoughts about race are so
significant to an understanding of *Cane*, I have quoted them from "On
Being an American" at length.

> Race is biological phenomenon. It has to do with the organic heredity, with the
> physical composition of people. ... At the same time, it is not possible to analyze
> the racial composition of a person as we analyze the chemical composition of a
> stone ... I may say of a given person that he is white or black, an oriental or an
> occidental; but what I say has no necessary relation to the nature and composi-
> tion of the person himself. On one hand we have actual racial composition; on
> the other hand we have my opinions about it together with whatever labels I
> may happen to use. ...

Now these labels, together with ideas, opinions, beliefs, emotions and their associated behavior constitute the sociological psychological factor of racial matters. ...

Thus for example, we may believe, and therefore assume it to be fact, that all of the main races are pure races. In point of fact all of the main races are mixed races—and so mixed that no one can unravel them in all of their blended races—and so mixed that no one can unravel them in all of their blended complexity. ...

In our own country it is comparatively simple to show the distinction between the racial and the sociological factors. There is a large group of people called "colored." Under this blanket label are to be found people with racial strains from every country on earth. Some of them are as white as anyone can be. The term "colored" obviously does not define their organic actuality. The term "colored" is a sociological psychological word which refers not to a racial but to a social group.

There is a larger grouping of people called white. As a matter of organic fact there are within the white group also racial strains from every race on earth. The racial or blood admixture is the organic actuality underlying the so-called white group. ...

By hearsay there were in my heredity the following strains: Scotch, Welsh, German, English, French, Dutch, Spanish, with some dark blood. For the point of this book, let us assume the dark blood was Negro—or let's be generous and assume that it was both Negro and Indian. I personally can readily assume this because I cannot feel with certain of my countrymen that all of the others are all right but the Negro is not. Blood is blood. ... Of what race am I? To this question there is and can be but one true answer—I am of the human race. ...

I was an American, neither white nor black, rejecting these divisions, accepting all people as people. ...

In my own mind I could not see the dark blood as something quite different and apart. But if people wanted to say this dark blood was Negro blood and if they then wanted to call me a Negro—this was up to them. Fourteen years of my life I had lived in the white group, four years I had lived in the colored group. In my experience there had been no main difference between the two. But if people wanted to isolate and fasten on those four years and to say that therefore I was colored, this too was up to them. ...

I determined what I would do. To my real friends of both groups, I would, at the right time, voluntarily define my position. As for people at large, naturally I would go my way and say nothing unless the question was raised. If raised, I would meet it squarely, going into as much detail as seemed desirable for the occasion. Or again, if it was not the person's business I would either tell him nothing or the first nonsense that came into head.

All of the while these thoughts were working out in my mind, my feelings little by little became outraged; my aristocracy might be invaded; I might be called to question by louts, white, black, or any other color. But as I settled the thing for myself and my mind grew quiet, my feelings quieted also.

Having been accepted as Euro-American all of his life, there was no point in Toomer insisting that he was African-American. His life as a Euro-American male in a Euro-American college began, with no trauma related to the legalities of segregation.

JEAN TOOMER'S LIFE PRIOR TO PUBLISHING *CANE*

Michael Krasny in "Jean Toomer's Life prior to *Cane:* A Brief Sketch of the Emergence of a Black Writer" agrees with Darwin Turner's analysis that Toomer wanted to settle in the South eventually and live as a gentleman planter, like his legendary father. This desire, Krasny says, guided his choice of a two-year agricultural degree program at the University of Wisconsin. However, in an autobiographical note to "Eight-Day World," Toomer, speaking of himself in the third person, writes, "He soon found he was not suited to be a farmer, scientific or otherwise." From several agricultural schools, Toomer moved to the Physical Training Center at the University of Chicago. (It should be noted that all of these schools were segregated in the early 1900s.) When Toomer encountered Darwinism and atheism at lectures given in the Loop in Chicago, he was converted to both theories.

Till then, I had believed in God, in the religious universe. Suddenly into my world came the ideas and facts of the naturalists and evolutionists. I read their books. I did a lot of thinking. With the result that my old world suddenly and completely collapsed, I found myself in a world without a God, I felt the foundations of the earth had been pulled from under me. I felt like a condemned man swinging with a rope about his neck.

Only a short while ago my political structures had been toppled. Now my religious ones were down also. In comparison with this experience, what did the courses at the University, or for that matter, anything, mean to me? ... I deliberately set about the forming of a buffer, of a protective mechanism, resolving to meet the world with, and to let it touch me only through, my mind. ...

No one knew what was happening to me. I dropped the University. I cut classes at College. I wasn't to be seen for several days.

Then, gradually, I began pulling myself together. Indeed, I swung into a period of intellectual activity such [as] I had never before even thought possible. I read and read. Not only books on socialism and evolution, but also novels.[12]

His friend Eleanor Davis, with whom he listened to the Loop lectures about such literary figures as George Bernard Shaw, Victor Hugo, and Walt Whitman, was probably the model for the character Bona in "Bona and Paul." Toomer's fascination with literature, philosophy, and art continued to grow, and he turned into a voracious reader.

At twenty-four Toomer was still living as a Euro-American male. Enrolling in a pre-law, social science program at a New York college, he listed his heritage as "French Cosmopolitan" on the admission forms. Although his brief contact with established African-American Harlem literary figures was not particularly important to his life or his later writing of *Cane,* what is important is that his university experience convinced him that he should abandon formal education and become a writer. After being disqualified for the draft, he spent 1919, 1920, and 1921 practicing his writing and working as an unsuccessful Ford salesman in Chicago, a substitute physical director in a college in Milwaukee, a store clerk in New York, a physical educational teacher and gym director for a university settlement on the East Side of New York, a fitter in the New Jersey shipyards, a nurse to his dying grandparents, and a theater manager. This latter experience, according to Krasny, helped provide the background for "Theater" and "Box Seat" in *Cane.* His stint as a grocery clerk likely affected his portrayal of Esther, who spent her whole life being a grocery clerk in her father's store.

In 1922 Toomer accepted a temporary position as principal in an industrial and agricultural school for African-Americans in Sparta, Georgia. He had finally come face-to-face with the life and legacy of his planter father and politician grandfather, and only "the shock of the South kept him going."[13] It was during this time, says Krasny, that Toomer "fixed upon the idea of an amalgam of his White and Black responses to life, the Caucasian and Negro blend in his own consciousness, in order to create a distinctly new 'essence' and art form." This study maintains that *Cane*'s design is both intentional and nonconventional as the first example of Toomer's attempt to invent a new form.

Waldo Frank prompted Toomer to write about the African-American experience. They toured the South together to gather material for separate books. Both books about African-Americans, *Cane* and *Holiday,* were published in 1923. Although Toomer was immersed in a world of Euro-American letters, his predilection for aesthetics and his obsession with the reality of having mixed blood drew him to explore concepts that became associated with the writers of the Harlem Renaissance. Perhaps this is the reason *Cane* makes the connection between race, sex, and class that illuminates the continuing struggle of African-Americans in the latter twentieth century and today so vividly.

Toomer was not attempting to define, affirm, or forward the cause of the "Negro" as political activist. The idea seems ludicrous when one realizes that he lived most of his life as a Euro-American. Toomer's designation as the father of the Harlem Renaissance reflects the immense importance of *Cane* as a model for African-American writers looking for new ways to portray the reality of the American racial dilemma. Toomer had broken the hold of traditional English literature on the African-American literary aesthetic. He offered a new structuring concept as an example of how to create a heretofore unrecorded vision of traditional African-American rural life and urban life in the segregated cities of the North during the Great Migration.

Cane supports the concept of an African-American aesthetic. For instance, there is something aesthetically different that separates *Cane* from Waldo Frank's novel *Holiday*. Larry Neal offers some reflections on the evolution of what he calls the Black Aesthetic in the twentieth century and mentions many of the elements that hold *Cane* together. Those elements center on a blending of the temporal and the nontemporal artistic forms in real life, religion, and race memory. It is Toomer's method of revealing race consciousness that separates *Cane* from works by Euro-American authors, such as Frank and Anderson, and unites him to other writers in the "Black Aesthetic" tradition.

> ... the folk spirit was walking in to die on the modern desert. The spirit was so beautiful. Its death so tragic. Just this seemed to sum [up] life for me. And this was the feeling I put into *Cane*. *Cane* was a swan song. It was a song of an end. And why no one has seen and felt that, why people have expected me to write a second and third and fourth book like *Cane*, is one of the queer misunderstandings of my life.[14]

CANE: THE DIVINE WORD OF THE HIGH PRIEST OF SOUL

In his dissertation "Jean Toomer's *Cane:* A Symbolistic Study," Paschal Jay Collins explores Jean Toomer's association with a group called "The New Patricians." The Patricians—Waldo Frank, Gorham Munson, Kenneth Burke, Hart Crane, and Jean Toomer—were exponents of Art as vision and were a minor avant-garde force proselytizing the principles of the Russian mystic P. D. Ouspensky. Collins says that Ouspensky had a profound influence on the form and content of *Cane*. Alice Poindexter Fisher argues the same point in her article "The Influence of Ouspensky's *Tertium Organum* upon Jean Toomer's *Cane*."

Fisher reviews the history of The Patricians' encounter with *Tertium Organum* and cites Waldo Frank as considering it to be their Bible. The major theories Fisher believes Toomer took from Ouspensky are as follows:

1. Time affects causality, motion, and dimension. The noumenal world is really the Eternal Now of Hindu philosophy—a universe in which there will be neither before nor after. There will be just one present known or unknown. Everything participates in eternity and is animated by a common energy source.
2. Our world is merely our incorrect perception of the world. We see the world as if we are looking through a narrow slit.
3. The nature of the world can really be known only through mysticism.
4. Only a poet can communicate both the mystical, emotional feelings of an experience and the concepts inherent in that experience.
5. Conceiving of one's artistic function as that of prophet and mythmaker inspires one to experiment radically with language and form in order to communicate that special insight.
6. If a rationality exists at all, it must exist in everything, including what we label inanimate or dead objects in nature. In other words, nature is animated by life and feeling everywhere and in everything. Individuality of thought and feeling is in everything.
7. Man's consciousness is divided into five parts: the intellectual, the emotional, the moving, the instinctual, and the sexual functions. The sexual functions are only important in that they serve as a measure of the development of the other of man's functions.
8. Man exists in a dreamlike condition.

Many of these ideas echo the traditional worldview of nature and man in the African and West Indian societies that were to influence the Negritude writers. Notably, Fisher points out the relationship between Ouspensky's notion of cause and effect and the cause and effect of the historic Atlantic Slave Trade that disrupted the evolution of African culture and the lives of Africana people throughout Africa. While Fisher applies this notion specifically to analyze "Carma," the Vertical Technique uses the same history to create a macrostructure from which one can view *Cane* and incorporate the other elements of Ouspensky's worldview.

Bernard Bell picks up this theme of the critical importance of the spiritual body to interpreting *Cane* in "Portrait of the Artist as the High Priest of Soul." Bell feels that "*Cane* marked the death of the Afro-American poet-realist and the birth of the Gurdjieffian high priest of soul."[15] Bell refers to the Gothic qualities of *Cane* and uses Biblical images and the religious quest as a basis of analysis. As he reviews the individual characters, Bell notes the differences between men and women. He identifies American racism as the modern-day Antichrist and suggests that Toomer's narrator sees women as the principle of receptivity and fertility, attempting to harmonize their physical drives with the psychic centers of their being and with the male principle. While this study sees the women's behavior of resistance within the structural meaning of the Vertical Technique, it does confirm Bell's analysis of Kabnis as the omniscient narrator, who cannot "harmonize" with any of the women, until he meets the healer, Carrie Kate.

In a different way Richard Eldridge in "The Unifying Images in Part One of Jean Toomer's *Cane*" relates the arcs in *Cane* to its structure and meaning. Theoretically, the arcs blend and overlap into one continuous circle to symbolize what Toomer calls the "circle design." The logic of the plot is character driven and not plot driven. Eldridge notes Toomer's rationale of the aesthetic relationship between the three parts, which move from a simple design to a complex design and back to a simple design again. The reality of the matter is that "Kabnis" is anything but simple, as the previous problems combined and are incorporated into the collection of characters in "Kabnis." This study has already noted the symbolic importance of the book moving geographically from the rural South to the urban South, to the North and then the far North and back to the rural South again—representing a major literary innovation in 1923.

By mapping *Cane*'s introductory arcs on the same page, a moonrise pattern appears that could not be seen except from someplace really high in the city or in the black of rural nightfall, where building lights could not interfere. Toomer's drawings can be seen as an attempt to record time phenomenologically. The visible degree of lunation in the phases of the moon, as it appears to us standing at a specific point on Earth, has been used by ancient poets and historians on many continents to mark the time of important moments in the life of the society and/or the person as oracular. Using a 2003 charting of lunation, the arcs of light (that a viewer would see from Earth that would correspond to the arc drawings—as points of lunar light) would indicate specific months and days, with the arc angle variance dependent on where you are standing. Universal Time or Greenwich Mean Time operates on astrological phenomena like Cyclical Phenomena Time. Toomer looked up and saw the moon in the south and north over a period longer than a year and noted the difference in its appearance. Often the November moon, also called the harvest moon or red moon, can be tracked through its change of color and full-ness during its ascension on the fall equinox. In reality, the moon is dark or black. What we see as light or color is its illumination by the sun. *Cane*'s structure itself is a metaphor for the mystical nature of the people described in its pages. After writing *Cane* (as a Gurdjieff fellow at the Priory at Avon near Fountainebleau in France), Toomer would spend a lot of time looking at the moon, having studied the writing and philosophy of Gurdjieff—as an Ouspensky teacher—during the period in which he wrote *Cane*.

Eldridge underscores John Reilly's argument in "The Reconstruction of Genre as Entry into Conscious History" and agrees with this study that says the unity of *Cane* is derived from a narrative structured by sequenc-ing images instead of the traditional Aristotelian unity of time, place, and conflict resolution. The unity of the book is not communicated by a tra-ditional central character with a single name but by an innovative evolv-ing narrator observer who wanders through the book changing form. Eldridge identifies the central images of the book as dusk, the moment of mystery, equipoise, and deep (purple) feeling; cane, the profound grip into the earth that nurtures life; and fermentation, the creative power that gives life purpose. He says that these images are oracular because the prophet-poet uses them to reveal the mystery of the spiritual life to those he thinks are in danger of losing it forever. Much of Eldridge's analysis agrees with the critical literature, but Eldridge uses Toomer's own com-mentary on *Cane* to ground his analysis. In the following quote, he intro-duces but does not develop a concept that is the foundation of the Vertical Technique:

> "There is one thing about the Negro in America which most thoughtful persons seem to ignore: The Negro is in solution, in the process of solution. As an entity, the race is losing its body, and its soul is approaching a common soul."[16]

The Vertical Technique puts all Africana people in the process of resolving a series of problems. Miraculously, *Cane* identifies and explores many of these problems still relevant in the twenty-first century.

The Vertical Technique takes a racial/historical view of *Cane*. Nevertheless, Toomer's delineations facilitate viewing the various parts of *Cane* in a variety of ways that make it possible to compare them to other American works.

Toomer insists on being seen as an essentialist. In "Earth-Being" Toomer says, "I am not a romanticist. I am an essentialist. Or, to put it in other words, I am a spiritualizer, a poetic realist."

In *Cane,* the protagonist allows himself (as Kabnis will not allow himself) to simply be a Euro-American/African-American artist creating what he must. The narrator has discovered and demonstrated that creativity and self-unity depend on each other, and both elements depend, ironically, on submission to the apparent chaos of the universe.

Ultimately, in "Jean Toomer's 'Blue Meridian'—The Poet as Prophet of a New Order of Man," Bernard Bell explains why he thinks Toomer was "more like the avant-garde of The Lost Generation, than the vanguard of the Harlem Renaissance." Toomer was deeply involved in creating a synthesis of new forms and themes. Attached to Walt Whitman, Robert Frost, and Sherwood Anderson, he also favored the Imagists' technique and philosophy.

"Blue Meridian" resolves the dilemma of how Toomer, through the Gurdjieff philosophy, unifies the parts of man—his mind, emotions, and body. Remember that Toomer has been raised in the Euro-American tradition that says those elements are separate. In contrast, Africana traditions consistently reify the natural unity of those three elements in a balanced human being. Toomer envisions America as Whitman does, "as the greatest poem," "a teeming nation of nations," and "the race of races." Toomer says in "Blue Meridian" that the three races (European, African, and Native American) have failed to "transform the soul of man." The new man will be an American, a unique species that represents, like Toomer, a synthesis of all races. Notice that this phase of Toomer's development happens before Franz Boas's anthropological studies are published, debunking the existence of different racial species on earth as a convenient mythology for Europe's expansionist motives. Afterward, science would prove conclusively that there is only one human race on the earth with different ethnic offshoots from an essentially African root.

To make the historical setting of "The Blue Meridian" clear, Bell mentions various historical events: Lindbergh has made his epic solo flight and Al Capone is a national figure. Several verses from "The Blue Meridian" (from Darwin Turner's authorized publication of Toomer's other works), in particular, concisely represent the subtle message of *Cane.*

> Unlock the races,
> Open this pod by outgrowing it,
> Free men from this prison and this shrinkage,
> Not from the reality itself
> But from out prejudices and preferences
> And the enslaving behavior caused by them,
> Eliminate these—
> I am, we are, simply of the human race.
> Uncase the nations,

Open this pod by outgrowing it,
Keep the real but destroy the false;
We are of the human nation.
Uncase the regions—
Occidental, Oriental, North, South—We are of Earth.
Free the sexes
From the penalties and proscriptions
That allegedly are laid on us
Because we are male and female.
Unlock the classes,
Emerge from those pockets;
I am, we are, simply of the human class ..."[17]

Eighty years later, a pop-rock group in blue face (The Blue Man Group with Dave Matthews) translates the dilemma of Toomer's "man of blue or purple" in 2003 in the song "Sing Along" on the compact disc *Complex*.

" ... If I tell you I'm strong
If I follow along
Will I keep feeling different ..."

CHAPTER 6

Intersecting Lines: Early Twentieth-Century Movements Touching Jean Toomer and Cane

HISTORICAL VIEW OF TOOMER AS HARLEM RENAISSANCE AND NEGRITUDE FATHER, WHO BECAME AN EX-NEGRO

E. Franklin Frazier in *The Negro Family in the United States* explains why a "Negro" cultural and artistic movement in the 1920s in America was critically important to the evolution of American culture. Jabulani Kamau Makalani uses Frazier's argument to link its necessity to

> the serious disruption and/or destruction of African cultural traditions, and insti-
> tutions, resulting from the historical experiences of colonialism, and the Middle
> Passage and chattel slavery. The [Negro] Renaissance symbolized the fact [that]
> the Black people in America, freed from the constraints of chattel slavery, were
> now able to seriously grapple with the question of culture (a way of life) and a
> collective direction for themselves. Blacks now had the opportunity to move
> into colleges and universities and for the first time to create a substantial intel-
> lectual class.[1]

The Renaissance was a response to historic events. Of these events, Walter White chronicles the Great Migration as the key element. This study believes that the second critical event was the advent of immigration from other Africana countries. As an anonymous writer describes it in *The Crisis:*

THE SHIFTING BLACK BELT

The department of labor has recently issued a report of its investigations on the migration of Negroes from the South in 1916 and 1917. The New York City Hotel Gazette summarizes:

Investigations of Negro migration to the North during the war, just issued by the Department of Labor, indicate that the total migration may have been as great as 350,000, extending over a period of about 18 months, during 1916 and 1917. That figure is fixed as the maximum limit, and 150,000 as the minimum limit, and the estimate of James H. Dillard, who had the charge of the inquiry, is 200,000.

The movement had been under way for a long time before any effort was made to determine the number of Negroes moving North. Moreover, so many left separately and unobserved that complete statistics would have been impracticable. The investigator in Georgia estimates that between 35,000 and 45,000 Negroes left that state in 1916–1917, and the number to leave Alabama during the same time is estimated at 75,000. State officials, however, made higher estimates, placing the number to leave Georgia at 50,000; Alabama, 90,000 and Mississippi 100,000.

Lack of labor in the North, due to the cessation of immigration, was the principal cause, the investigators agree. Among the causes operative in the South to induce migration were general dissatisfaction with conditions, the ravages of the boll-weevil, floods, change of crop system, low wages, poor housing, poor schools, unsatisfactory crop settlements, rough treatment, cruelty of the law officer, unfairness in court procedure, lynchings, desire to travel, labor agents, aid from Negroes in the North, and the influence of the Negro press.

The movement of large numbers at the same time was due largely to labor agents, but after these initial group movements, Negroes kept going North in small numbers, attracted by the letter from their friends who had already gone. Better wages were important. "Every Negro who made good in the North, started a new group on the way," one of the investigators reported.[2]

The Great Migration was a rapid, continuous flow of African-Americans from the southern states to the North beginning in 1860. The boll weevil infestation that sharply reduced cotton production (most African-Americans worked in the cotton industry) created the need for great numbers of African-Americans to find new work. So one primary mission of the migration was economic. Initially, the southern status quo, as represented by the southern press, was very happy about this. "They felt that the old doctrine of settling race relations by deporting Negroes to Africa, long since abandoned by sensible persons, might be of value still and that the journey North was but one step toward ridding America of the vicious, indolent and criminal blacks."[3] However, when northern industries began to recruit and pay African-American labor and the South began to realize the economic implications of not having neoslave labor to support the southern economy, southern newspapers began a massive propaganda campaign to scare African-Americans into staying in the "safe" south. Nevertheless, the flow of labor continued toward the Chicago stockyards and railroads, the Pittsburgh steel mills, Detroit automobile factories, and elsewhere in the North.

Although one of the primary causes of the Great Migration was the need to work, an equal need to be "safe" also motivated African-Americans to leave the South. In the 1890s, Ida B. Wells carefully documented lynching as a tool of economic terrorism in America's racial class war. African-Americans were fleeing the South for the unknown. This included leaving England's ex–prison colony settlement, the state of Georgia, where, out of the 3,436 persons who were known to have been lynched throughout America, 429 of them had been lynched in Georgia between January 1,1889, and January 1, 1921.[4] Lynching was a big business and an accepted ritualized group activity in the Euro-American South. African-Americans migrated north in an attempt to save their lives, as much as they migrated to create better lives for themselves.

Migrating north also presented the possibility of escaping Jim Crow segregation that both restricted and limited the African-American in every area of life in the South and was enforced by representatives of the US system of law. Of course, caste and class in the North, along with more subtle, sophisticated segregation/racism, kept African-Americans effectively segregated till the 1960s. Harlem became the "housing haven" because there were a limited number of choices available to African-Americans moving to New York. The efforts of Euro-Americans to hold back African-American expansion in Harlem was unsuccessful because no single organization was able to gain total support of all the Euro-American property owners in Harlem. It was a mistake Euro-American communities would learn from and not make again. However, once the "takeover" of Harlem was complete, it was obviously not a ghetto just because African-Americans (instead of Euro-Americans) lived there. That had never been its social architect's intention.

Harlem was a cultural jewel—a model of prosperity and elegance to be imitated. It was not a slum but rather a place where African-Americans had reasonable-to-decent housing options in a respected neighborhood. All kinds of African-Americans lived there: That included a substantial bourgeois class, a proletariat class, a criminal underworld, and an academic intellectual class, all of which were sustained within Harlem's borders. If this description does not make it obvious that Harlem's African consciousness was part and parcel of its political consciousness, the work of Marcus Garvey makes this point absolutely clear. His philosophy represents one impact of the Atlantic Slave Trade on the development of an Africana people throughout the diaspora. It focuses on establishing and maintaining new direct links to Africa in the twentieth century.

The timing of the Universal Negro Movement Association was strategically brilliant in orchestrating its success in America. (It had failed in Jamaica where Garvey was born.) Cynicism, resulting from the broken government promises of the post–World War I period, was epidemic. African-Americans were losing faith in their ability to overcome their historic position in American society and the institutionalization of racism. Adam Clayton Powell, Jr. wrote of Garvey, saying, "Marcus Garvey was one of the greatest mass leaders of all time. He was misunderstood and maligned, but he brought to the Negro people for the first time a sense of pride in being black."[5] Garvey's cry of "Up You Mighty Race!" was a call to arms of people of African descent. Either they acknowledged their shared tradition or denied it for another. There was no middle ground.

The Negro World was a newspaper dedicated to the concerns of Africana people, and Garvey used it to voice his opinions on the importance of acknowledging Africa as the African-Americans' homeland.[6] The Garvey Movement had a profound effect on the political development of Harlem and the lives of Adam Clayton Powell, Sr. and Jr. The fight to make Harlem a congressional district began during the Garvey period. By 1929 Garvey had become a world figure because his movement was one rational response to the years of neglect, suppression, and degradation that many people of African descent all over the world had experienced. The movement had indigenous roots and could have existed without the concern and interest of Europeans or Euro-Americans. The attempt to project the positive progression of the dark-skinned peoples inhabiting the New World was a momentous task. Garvey's attempt was so successful that it became necessary for the US government to stop him. (This systemic response to African-American leadership would be reinstituted with the rise of Malcolm X.) As might be expected, the Garvey Movement began to fragment and decline concurrently with the end of the Harlem Renaissance. This occurred just as the Negritude Movement was being born in Europe.

The message of the literature of the Harlem Renaissance was a strategic answer to all the economic, political, philosophical, and cultural forces at work in Harlem. Alain Locke, architect of the Harlem

Renaissance and creator of "The New Negro" as a philosophical construct, described the literary movement during this period:

> The Younger Generation comes, bringing its gifts. They are the first fruits of the Negro Renaissance. Youth speaks and the voice of the New Negro is heard. ...
>
> Negro genius today relies upon the race-gift as a vast spiritual endowment from which our best developments have come and must come. Racial expression as a consciousness motive, it is true, is fading out of our latest art, but just as surely the age of true, finer group expression is coming in—for race expression does not need to be deliberate to be vital. Indeed at its best it never is. ...
>
> The younger generation has achieved an objective attitude toward life. Race for them is but an idiom of experience, a sort of added enriching adventure and discipline, giving subtler overtones to life, making it more beautiful and interesting, even if more poignantly so. So experienced, it affords a deepening rather than a narrowing of social vision. The artistic problem of the Young Negro has not been so much that of acquiring the outer mastery of form and technique as that of acquiring the inner mastery of mood and spirit. ... Our poets no longer have the hard choice between an over-assertive and an appealing attitude. By the same effort they have shaken themselves free from the minstrel tradition and the fowling-nets of dialect, and through acquiring ease and simplicity in serious expression, have carried the folk-gift to the altitudes of art. There they seek and find art's intrinsic values and satisfactions—and if America were deaf, they would still sing.
>
> ... Then, rich in this legacy, but richer still, I think, in their own endowment of talent, comes the youngest generation of our Afro-American culture: in music, Diton, Dett, Grant Still, and Roland Hayes; in fiction, Jessie Fauset, Walter White, Claude McKay (a forthcoming book); in drama, Willis Richardson; in the field of the short story, Jean Toomer, Eric Walrond, Rudolph Fischer; and finally a vivid galaxy of young Negro poets, McKay, Jean Toomer, Langston Hughes and Countee Cullen.
>
> These constitute a new generation not because of years only, but because of a new aesthetic and a new philosophy of life.[7]

Langston Hughes phrases this literary declaration of independence more aggressively in "The Negro Artist and the Racial Mountain," published prominently in *The Nation*.

> One of the most promising of the young Negro poets said to me once, "I want to be a poet—not a Negro poet," meaning, I believe, "I want to write like a white poet": meaning subconsciously, "I would like to be a white poet"; meaning behind that, "I would like to be white." And I doubted then that, with his desire to run away spiritually from his race, this boy would ever be a great poet. But this is the mountain standing in the way of any true Negro art in America—this urge within the race toward whiteness, the desire to pour racial individuality

into the mold of American standardization, and to be as little Negro and as much American as possible.

... The road for the serious black artist, then, who would produce a racial art is most certainly rocky and the mountain is high. Until recently he received almost no encouragement for his work from either white or colored people. ...

... Both would have told Jean Toomer not to write *Cane*. The colored people did not praise it. The white people did not buy it. Most of the colored people who did read *Cane* hated it. They are afraid of it. Although the critics gave it good reviews the public remained indifferent. Yet (excepting the work of Du Bois) *Cane* contains the finest prose written by a Negro in America. And like the singing of Robeson, it is truly racial.

... We younger Negro artists who create now intend to express our individual dark-skinned selves without fear or shame. If white people are pleased we are glad. If they are not, it doesn't matter. We know we are beautiful. And ugly too. The tom-tom cries and the tom-tom laughs. If colored people are pleased we are glad. If they are not, their displeasure doesn't matter either. We build our temples for tomorrow, strong as we know how and we stand on top of the mountain, free within ourselves.[8]

Eugene C. Holmes's article "Alain Locke and the New Negro Movement" attempts both to define the Harlem Renaissance and to put it in the proper historical perspective. The New Negro writers were not centered only in Harlem, and much of the best writing of the decade was not always done in Harlem. (Most of the writers were not Harlemites. Nevertheless, Harlem money and cultural institutions played an important role in providing a meeting ground for writers of African descent, from all over the world.) Holmes says that the New Negro had temporal roots in the past and spatial roots elsewhere in America. The American literary tradition was being revised for use by the African-American writer. Locke recognized and encouraged the literary evolution of the Harlem Renaissance.

The relationship between American industrialization and the New Negro is a matter of the historical record. That record consolidates industry as monopoly capitalism on production—on a global scale: the varied and cheap market products to which Americans grew addicted. This was conducted by Euro-American capitalists utilizing cheap African-American and immigrant labor, unlimited natural resources, and heretofore unequaled technology for marketing products globally. It was this creation of capital that led to the emergence of America as a preeminent economic and military force early in the twentieth century.

Holmes reaffirms Toomer's disposition on the need for a national literature, in the development of a cultural democracy in America. Holmes refers to *Cane* as a part of the literary tradition that Locke was cultivating. The Negritude Movement was to share the same focus on Africana pride and Black Nationalism as the Harlem Renaissance. It began about the time the Harlem Renaissance started to decline, as a geographically located movement in 1930.

BRIEF REVIEW OF THE NEGRITUDE MOVEMENT

Negritude, it is this distant tom-tom in the nocturnal streets of Dakar, it is the voodoo cries of the Haitian worshipper which slide to the edge of the precipice, it is the Congo mask.[9]

Along with Aimé Cesairé and Leon Damas, one of three fathers of the Negritude Movement (poet, soldier, scholar, and ex-President of Senegal—politician, statesman, ideologist, and world diplomat), Leopold Sedar Senghor defines Negritude as a cultural movement. Martha Louise Climo cited Senghor in his *Imagery: An Expression of His Negritude:*

... [It] is the awareness, defence and development of African cultural values. ... It is the awareness by a particular social group of people of its own situation in the world, and the expression of it by means of a concrete image.[10]

In an article titled "Trois poetes negro-americains," published in Paris in *Poesie 45 23:33,* Senghor articulates the concept of an Africana people for the first time, identifying the work of the three African-American poets (in Michel Fabre's words in *Black American Writers in France 1840-1980*) "as the mark of a cosmic and human inspiration with a unique rhythm." Earlier at the 1900 Paris Exposition, W. E. B. Du Bois curated a striking photographic exposition juxtaposing visual images of the spectrum of African-American appearance that functionally critiqued the science of race proliferating at the change of the century. Chike Onwuachi, the first director of the Black Studies Program at Washington University in St. Louis, Missouri, proposed the following definition of Negritude:

Negritude is saying that the African world is the world of man ... characterized by spiritual and economic communalism, collective human consciousness and humanistic-orientated development ... the problematic issue of Negritude is not definition but actional translation. Whether it is Negritude or African personality, we African people are dealing with ethno-psychological problems rather than melanic problems. It is the issue of the right attitude toward Black existential postulates and their objective resolution.[11]

These two definitions echo Alain Locke's and W. E. B. Du Bois's statements about the Harlem Renaissance. More importantly, the Negritude

Movement was a reaction to the same forces that made the Great Migration necessary and forced Harlem into becoming the temporary stronghold of Africana culture and politics. In the early 1930s African, African-American, and West Indian students who migrated to Paris to study began to question France's policy of assimilation in its colonies. France assumed the revolutionary doctrine of the equality of man but practiced the superiority of European man, and specifically French civilization and culture, over peoples of color. Led by Aimé Césaire of Martinique, the students began to assert themselves as Africans in the same ways "Negroes" began to assert themselves as African-Americans in America. In 1934, Senghor founded the journal *L'Etudiant Noir,* which gave the students a channel for self-expression that would resound all over the world.

In both movements, the creation of a literature to voice and record the philosophy was crucial. African intellectuals created the Negritude Movement in Paris, France; African-American intellectuals created the Harlem Renaissance Movement in Harlem, New York (a predominantly Euro-American state in a predominantly Euro-American country). Both movements struggled to survive in the midst of the elements against which they were fighting. They intellectualized and ritualized the lives of the villagers and rural folk in Africa or "down south" in America. They turned colonialism, imperialism, and racism into art to confront the problems of the twentieth century—what Onwauchi calls

> the problem of the socio-political implications of color as it relates to the issues of existence between the colonizers from the European world and the colonized from the African world. It is the essential question surrounding the issue of the value of living and the characteristic style of Black existence based on the very essence of being Black ... the essence of Negritude must be articulated in Afrocentricism, the perspective in which the Black man is objectively translated in his true essence of being a whole-man and not as a pathological adjunct of the white man, not as the invisible man in the white dominated world. The ideology of Negritude can best be realized if we can focus on what the Black People have in common all over the world (that is the white problem) rather than focus on what divides the Black people as human beings.[12]

As a philosophical construct, Negritude continues to be identified primarily with Aimé Césaire, Leopold Sedar Senghor, and Leon Damas. Nevertheless, other African writers have contributed greatly to the development of a literature of Negritude. Senghor, as past president of Senegal, has been primarily responsible for spreading the philosophy of Negritude throughout the Africana diaspora. The Negritude Movement's aim is identical to that of the philosophy of the Harlem Renaissance, as conceived by Alain Locke. In regards to their literature, Negritude writers use more innovations, more nontraditional methods of organizing images to present the African worldview than the Harlem Renaissance writers. However, the goals of both movements are the same. From the very inception of the Negritude Movement, its leaders recognized a unity among all Africans on the continent of Africa, regardless of language or geographical locations, as well as Africans in the New World. Indeed, Senghor acknowledges the Negritude Movement's debt to the Harlem Renaissance and specifically to Jean Toomer, who in a different way, shared their dilemma of the divided self.

> I am pleased to render homage here to the pioneer thinkers who lighted our path in the years 1930-1935; Alain Locke, W. E. B. Du Bois, Marcus Garvey, Carter G. Woodson. And also to pay well-deserved tribute to the poets whose works we translated and recited, and in whose footsteps we tried to follow: Claude McKay, Jean Toomer, Countee Cullen, James Weldon Johnson, Langston Hughes, Sterling Brown.[13]

CANE'S RELEVANCE TO THE HARLEM RENAISSANCE AND THE NEGRITUDE MOVEMENT

Jean Toomer's *Cane* is important to both of these movements because its artistry clearly shapes the definition of man in literature (in eloquent deft language merging the power of a blues song with the technology of the molded imagery of naturalism); it establishes the importance of literature as a bi-dialectical, international tool for the enlightenment of Africana peoples everywhere. Toomer's poems in *Cane* are among the first work to be translated and discussed fervently. Literature is important in these philosophical political discussions, leading to major political and social revolutions, because of a simple biological fact. The human organism only "knows" the world through symbolic representations, processed through its morphology and neurological systems. Human beings *are* the world and *in* the world simultaneously. The information that one is given or experiences determines one's definition of what or who is human in the world and what constitutes humane behavior, something Gurdjieff helps Toomer rationalize after he writes *Cane*. However, Ouspensky's sense of the relationship of sign and symbols' impact on consciousness permeates *Cane,* from Toomer's early encounters with Ouspensky's disciples. It's the reason why *Cane* does not proselytize the reader, even in its gruesome moments. Toomer realizes that he is giving the reader a window to see into the reality surrounding their body by primarily using other bodies. This writing methodology is a priori in the same way his study "of doing" at the priory in Avon continues to develop his thinking in this direction.

Cane shows us life in America—in Georgia, in Washington, D.C., in Chicago—as it was in the early twentieth century; not as it is represented currently or as mainstream American history has represented it before revisionist history. *Cane* redefines the diverse reality of American racism and terrorism in the 1920s and suggests that the American class structure (based on race), is beyond logic—it is anti-body and antilife and can only be changed at the level of the individual mind by systemically reevaluating the definition of what a human being is within the reality of American racism in that era. *Cane* presents a coherent process "of doing" by reading to challenge the individual to make the journey to change only to the extent that the individual's ability allows.

The Atlantic Slave Trade marks the beginning of the period of the modern world, and it is one of the major forces that generates the wealth of Europe and America and shapes its definition of man. Before the advent of the slave trade, the African is revered, honored for his intellect, practical arts (such a medicine), and fine art. (See *Africa and Africans As Seen by Classical Writers* by William Leo Hansberry.[14]) Before the advent of the Atlantic Slave Trade, the historic definition of man in England is very simple: Man = Free Man = Patriarch, who rules society as Father. The exceptions to the rule are European women of immediate royal bloodline. After the advent of the Atlantic Slave Trade, the definition changes in Europe and in the Americas to: Man = Man of European Descent Exclusively = Free Man = Patriarch, who rules society as Father; there were no exceptions for European women of any bloodline in the New World. In the vocabulary of Joseph Conrad's 1897 novel *The Nigger of the "Narcissus,"* niggers became the absolute other in human society, and their value could only be determined by their worth as capital or usefulness to the economic machinery. Niggers had no history, no people, no geographic placement. Niggers in Paris in 1921 were an oddity, a tool of colonialism. Edward Braithwaite delineates the history of this transformation succinctly in "Race and the Divided Self."

> America, North and South, was once inhabited and was being civilized by a people, the "Amerindians," who had come to assume it as their own. That was until Columbus and the European intrusion of the sixteenth century. After that, especially in the northern continent, the indigenous population was destroyed or confined, the "palefaces" took over, and to replace the labor rejected by or disallowed to the Indians, several millions of Africans were imported to the New World as slaves. These three factors—the destruction of the Indians, the domination of Europe and the enormity of slavery—are central experiences of the American hemisphere. The destruction of the aboriginal culture removed a vital

local norm or model which in turn posed tremendously exacting problems for the newcomers. European technology came into head-on confrontation with forest and frontier, creating a kind of alter-Renaissance personality: energetic, versatile, materialistic. It was the domination of this variation of European constellation at that place and time that made of slavery the horror it became; for to justify it, the Atlantic European had to develop theories of race and racial superiority unknown to neoplatonists or Galileo. Out of this has come the North America of Ford, Carnegie, Rockefeller, Apollo multi-million-dollar moonshots; Watts, Chicago's Southside, Harlem, the Soledad Brothers, Panthers, Attica: white/wealth, Black/ poverty, outer exploration and interior hate.[15]

Outer exploration and inner hate describe Kabnis's sojourn through the world of *Cane*. He objectively and subjectively examined the other humans in his environment in the South and North, only to have to face his own ugliness—his own dilemma—his own definition of man through, "My ancestors were Southern Bluebloods." The dilemma of the twentieth century remains unsolved in the twenty-first. The problem of the color line advances with technology with us. *Cane* states that problem, its cause, and its results in a nonaggressive manner and thus provides a medium for generating a dialogue in the classroom between men and women of all races.

Anthropologist Jules Henry insists that American schools are institutions for drilling students in cultural orientation. He singles out education as the greatest paradox of the human condition because learning to learn is humankind's most formidable evolutionary task. Providing for the conservation of culture—while executing changes in it to secure its survival—challenges humanity's need to make certain of its survival as opposed to the probability of successful adaptations. "The function of education has never been to free the mind and the spirit, but to bind them."[16]

Dr. Henry's analysis is relevant to this study because it describes intellectually creative children that continually fail in school because they cannot understand (in Henry's words) the "stupidities" they are taught to believe as facts that are not scientific facts or truths grounded in concrete reality. These children, who are perfectly normal and bright, find it impossible to learn—that is, to memorize the absurdities as knowledge—and difficult to accept the assigned authority of those absurdities as a way of life. Finding themselves surrounded in school by people who think that they are absurd or stupid, these students usually come to think of themselves as stupid.

Toomer's literary innovation in *Cane* is startling as a challenge to the logic of style and content in American letters. As a work of art, it also challenges the absurdities that Toomer enumerates with care in his autobiographical writings. *Cane* can provide a way of discussing the current American dilemma of race and class and introduce the importance of literature as a repository of culture as it is or was in 1923.

Schools are the final bastion of racism. Schools, or rather the instructors who work in them, teach people to remain separate and unequal. Therefore, it is in the schools that we must attack the problem of redefining both man and mankind through a controlled curriculum to functionally include Conrad's "absolute other." African-Americans are still struggling today for what the US Constitution promises all—equality of economic opportunity, equality of justice: equality of manner of worship—as American citizens engage the monolithic body of worshippers of the Islamic faith, which unites a great many Africans in the New World and in the Old World. As in 1923, Toomer has also provided a challenge to use *Cane* to try to see our way to peace on earth or be lost in a deadly war where the illogic of racism and sexism prevails over the inherited god-spirit of humankind.

HISTORICAL CONTEXT AND THE SEARCH FOR SELF

Toomer was surrounded by massive change in the early 1920s. One of those changes was America's takeover of global drug trafficking. Alfred McCoy, in *The Politics of Heroin: CIA Complicity in the Global Drug Trade*, notes with alarming detail how the global narcotics trade has been shaped by the traffic in opium and heroin (its modern derivative) and how the 1949 rise of the Communist Party in China effectively eradicated mass narcotic addiction and the world's largest source of opium. For most of its four thousand years of recorded history, opium remained limited in both its production and use. It was neither a popular or accessible drug until the nineteenth century, when consumption rose dramatically in both Asia and the West, particularly the United Kingdom and the United States. The European pharmaceutical industry created and marketed the morphine derivative acetic anhydride. In 1898, the Bayer Corporation created and marketed diacetylmorphine (also called heroin) as a cure for infant respiratory ailments. In 1899, a related analgesic derivative was developed and marketed as "aspirin."

> Historian David Musto has estimated that there were three hundred thousand American opium and heroin addicts in 1900—primarily women. At that time, women were banned from barrooms and confined to a nurturing role, so this highly addictive drug marketed as a treatment for children's ailments was a natural for them. You can find an evocative and accurate depiction of this problem in Eugene O'Neill's classic play "Long Day's Journey into Night," about his own mother's addiction.[17]

McCoy's discussion of the politics and statistics of drug addiction in the United States in the early 1900s provides the reader of *Cane* with a startling historical fact that can be related to the "listlessness" of many of the women characters and their indifferent attitude toward both people and events in the stories and poems. The facts of the period suggest that they were not only politically oppressed but an effective method of control over their lives had been established in the sale of heroin and aspirin. With one exception—Carma in overalls, strong as any man—none of them rebel, protest, or say very much in comparison to the male narrator. Toomer means *Cane* to be an observational work, where he shows the reader what he understands about life in the 1920s. If we thought they were somehow caricatures, more and more readers have come to understand to what extent the characters reflect people who really lived during that period.

In the same way, another powerful element of change in Toomer's environment was the idea of enfranchising women as a way of improving the overall society. The September 1912 issue of the NAACP magazine *The Crisis* argued that the suffrage map of the United States only contained six states—California, Washington, Colorado, Wyoming, Utah, and Idaho—and that the argument against the right of all adults (of any skin hue) being able to vote was impeding the progress of the country. Adella Hunt Logan in "Colored Women as Voters" says:

> More and more colored women are studying public questions and civics. As they gain information and have experience in their daily vocations and in their efforts for human betterment they are convinced, as many other women have long ago been convinced, that their efforts would be more telling if women had the vote.

Toomer's men in *Cane* are aware of the handicap that they have over the women and yet they often express helplessness and a desire for various levels and kinds of bonding with the women, who must have at least heard the argument for suffrage for Euro-American women and wondered about their own rights.

Ultimately, what *Cane*'s men appear to want is to be in a better state than the one they are in. They want to be stronger and more powerful to do the things that they believe men should do. The evolving narrator, but not all of the other male characters, seems to be aware of Ouspensky's delineation of the four states of being: sleep, waking state, self-consciousness and objective consciousness. They all have some sense of "the third state of self-consciousness or occasional moments of self-consciousness, leaving vivid memories of the circumstances that accompany them but no command over them." Toomer's characters seem to want to enter a state of objective consciousness where they would have control over their memories and their ability to learn from them: but they cannot. Only Kabnis, with Carrie Kate's assistance, sees the light of illumination in the distance. Ouspensky's concept of the universe was another wind of change sweeping the beginning of the twentieth century, one that would later become formalized in his published writings.

Toomer says in his article, "Why I Entered Gurdjieff Work," that his best talent is his ability to analyze things and see them for what they really are at this level of reality. "One's highest gift should be utilized until one has attained a faculty that is higher than it. It seemed to me that if I possessed any gift at all it was that of psychological thinking and understanding."[18]

One way to see *Cane* is to see Toomer at the beginning of understanding Ouspensky's definition of psychology as self-study, where he must study himself and his people as one studies a complicated machine of unknown potential. Ouspensky believed that man was a machine in denial of being a machine with seven functions: (1) thinking or intellect; (2) feelings or emotions; (3) instinctive function or all outer work of the organism; (4) movement in space; (5) sex or the function of two principles, male and female, in all of their manifestations; (6) higher emotional function or higher state of self-consciousness; and (7) higher mental function or the state of objective consciousness. In the *Psychology of Man's Possible Evolution,* Ouspensky says that man rarely attains these last two functional states and can only learn about them indirectly from those who have attained or experienced them.

Ouspensky's 1913 book, *The Symbolism of the Tarot: Philosophy of Occultism in Pictures and Numbers,* was a far cry away from Henry Ford's idea of controlling the country's destiny by mechanizing it, even at a personal level. Ouspensky had already stated that man was a highly evolved machine that needed to train to use all of his parts in a more efficient manner and thus achieve a higher level of awareness and a higher quality of life. A "special mind is necessary" to comprehend the symbolic language of the universe talking to us individually. Part of the training of this mind was developing the facility to manipulate and interpret the Tarot, "the most complete code of Hermetic symbolism [that] we [humans] possess." Toomer's primary structural concept in the three arcs is an innovation on Ouspensky's "Triangle as God" concept. He taught the triangle as God the Trinity or a concrete symbol for the world of ideas or the noumenal world. The point in the center of the triangle is man's soul, which, having no dimension in the world of the spirit, is symbolized by the surrounding triangle, enclosed in a square, the phenomenal world (of the senses). Toomer uses this concept to develop nonlinear characterizations that work at revealing the soul of the persona. In this work he would also have encountered the word *Kabala* as the high order of Judaic mysticism and with the prefix *Kab-* in Kabalist, who believes that every phenomenon consists of the name of God as The Word or Logos.

The four cycles of Vertical Technique can be seen as a transmutation of the four elements or the four principles forming the symbol for God for Kabalists.

> The world in itself, as the Kabalists hold, consists of four elements, or the four principles forming O n e . These four principles are represented by the four letters of the name of Jehovah. The basic idea of the Kabala consists in the study of the N a m e   o f   G o d   in its manifestation. Jehovah in Hebrew is spelt by four letters, Y o d ,   H e ,   V a u ,   a n d   H e —I. H. V. H. To these four letters is given the deepest symbolic meaning. The first letter expresses the a c t i v e   p r i n c i p l e , the beginning o r the first cause, motion, energy {I}; the second letter expresses the p a s s i v e element, inertia, quietude, {not I}: the third, the b a l a n c e   o f   o p p o s i t e s , {form}; and the fourth, the r e s u l t   o r   l a t e n t   e n e r g y .

> The Kabalists affirm that every phenomenon and every object consists of these four principles, i.e., that every object and every phenomenon consists of the Name of God (The Word),—L o g o s .[19]

Tarot symbolism also intersects with other popular works at the beginning of the century.

Another elemental model of writing in Toomer's environment is the writing of Max Jacob, described as a hypersensitive Jew turned Christian—with Picasso as a godfather—a student of astrology, numerology, and the Kabbala. Jacob was an art critic turned poet, who was born in Quimper in Celtic Brittany and who moved to Paris to study painting. As a protégé to Picasso, who believed in the genius of his poetry, Jacob, in league with Guillaume Apollinaire, would establish a "new spirit of modern" in poetry. Apollinaire published his first book. Jacob's book, published by the famous art dealer Daniel-Henry Kahnweiler, was illustrated by Picasso. The two artists worked in tandem through developing a new way of seeing image in the Western tradition of thought, though not necessarily in other Africana cultures. This new way of seeing would be called Cubism first and then Surrealism. Jacob's work with the schizophrenic prose poem, beginning in 1903, would be a poetic voice for the visual work leading these artistic movements. "Moon Poem" evokes the visual feeling of *Cane*'s poetry without replicating any of the same images.

Moon Poem

> At night three mushrooms are the moon. Abruptly as a cuckoo clock striking, they rearrange themselves each month at midnight. In the garden are rare flowers, little men lying down, a hundred of them, reflections in a mirror. In my dark room a luminescent censor is prowling, then two ... phosphorescent air ships, reflections in a mirror. In my head a bee is talking.

Le cornet a des[20]

Editor and translator William Kulik in *The Selected Poems of Max Jacob* uses a footnote citation which links Jacob's concept of writing to Toomer's concept of organization in *Cane* and Ouspensky's philosophy.

> Art as an expression of will was essential to Jacob—"the will to exteriorize oneself by chosen means." In a 1936 letter, Max elaborated on the definition using the image of one ellipse inside another: "I'm in the middle (Max Jacob), I have my subject, which circles the ellipse, at first near me, then further ... and further ... it almost disappears but I observe it, as it comes back to me. I am always at the center: *it is necessary to direct and not be directed* ... to attract the reader and sometimes lose him one can make the subject 'leap' to a second ellipse and reverse direction."[21]

Jacob's work was a part of the global environment of ideas available through books to Toomer. Jacob's use of poetry as an investigation of the emotional range of man (between ecstasy and disillusion) was a pioneering exploration of a psychological approach to literature, not unlike Toomer's. Jacob died in a Nazi concentration camp in 1944; his publications have left an indelible mark on the nature and the history of modern literature.

Another remarkable kind of schizophrenic, psychological, racial literature would also be present in 1921. The work of H. P. Lovecraft in the short story "The Nameless City" would literally spawn a whole new genre of horror/fantasy writing challenging the limits of the western literary imagination. The publication of his enthralling terrifying tales in *Weird Tales* magazine would establish him as a major vernacular literary figure and a writer who had effectively altered modern reality forever around the archives of "Miskatonic University."

Lovecraft's idea of alternative education in what would later be named the Cthulu Mythos (in honor of one of the major monster horrors in his stories) is the kind of house of learning that might have attracted Toomer. Like Toomer's writing, Lovecraft's work deconstructs the image and the ideology of conventional reality. What both Jacob's and Lovecraft's work have in common is the concept that becoming a highly developed man of knowledge was critical to surviving the illusion of life.

Supporting Ouspensky's concept of developing a highly evolved man was a popular 1894 memoir/novel about an evolved couple called *Brother of Third Degree* by Will L. Garver, published by the Borden Publishing Company located then in Alhambra, California. It detailed the process of the rise of a married couple through the esteemed masonic ranks to the then mystical and esoteric state of the Third Degree. The narrator teacher talks about how both the supplicants and the readers (as potential supplicants) must control their thoughts, for every thought that we think forms a corresponding condition in your mind and body. The narrator precedes modern motivational philosophy in saying, "Thoughts are more powerful and potent than acts"—that in our reality thoughts come first; we are built up of our own thoughts and we are surrounded by invisible powers that are given strength or weakened by these thoughts. The memoir/novel revealing man's more fantastical existence as a being on earth teaches (in 1894) that the one brotherhood is humanity and that "the sum total of the individualized centers of the divine activity, which while apparently separate, are one in life and essence."

Cane's narrator seems to be thinking aloud—most of the time—for everyone. It is as if he were trying to help the reader to enter a state of objective consciousness to better understand the truth of the matter in *Cane* that says every man is an individualized manifestation of God in self-imposed conditions. Man is "a center in the Infinite Essence around which the spirit vibrates and through which it flows forth and reveals itself in the world of forms and things." Toomer declared all men flawed and sacred in *Cane*, as the reader watches them working out their possible evolution. If much of *Cane*'s politics is poised on love relationships or partnerships involving coitus, it takes another dominant concept from the novel *Brother of the Third Degree* that suggests that the desire to love was man's soul's desire for a portion of itself which was lost and without which it would always be incomplete. One of the functions of the women of *Cane* is to represent the various aspects of the body's seven functions. The men's attempts to unite with or control the women are attempts to unify themselves toward the goal of full human enfranchisement—full life.

That other corollary literary and cultural movements should have the same goal during the early twentieth century is not surprising. What is remarkable is that the same few African-Americans would steer the philosophical course of those movements with no official title, financial endowment, or institutional approval. Langston Hughes was a critical change element of life throughout the Africana Diaspora in 1921, two years before the appearance of *Cane*. Hughes would link both Francophone and Latin American Africana movements to the Harlem Renaissance and to African Negritude, and in his role as facilitator bring that knowledge to everyone in each of the geographically separate environments. In the following excerpt from *Langston Hughes: Six Letters to Nicolas Guillen,* we see him tailor "Negrismo," which stylistically is much closer to *Cane* than all other major works of the early Harlem Renaissance by African-American writers.

Man! Your *Motivos de Son* are stupendous! They are at once very Cuban and very good ... I like them all ... And be careful not to write new *Motivos* too hastily. Give them time to grow into your heart ... But they are so good, the first *Motivos*, that all the ones that follow will have to be as good, or better. And poems are not written because the public wants them, but because the poet is ready to sing.[22]

Lesley Feracho in "The Legacy of Negrismo/Negritude: Inter-American Dialogues" makes the same difficult argument for Afro-Latin writers that others made for *Cane* in saying, "Negrismo's greatest difficulty lay in the very representation of Blacks" that its writers presented. In both cases, the images were still congruent with the literary stereotypes of Europeans and Euro-Americans. Feracho uses Richard Jackson's theory in *Black Literature and Humanism in Latin America* to substantiate his objections.

To begin with, as a minimum we must acknowledge that the movement had two faces (negrismo and negritude), understand that there was a clear distinction between two concepts, and recognize the often paradoxical roles of the movement's leading participants and indeed of the movement itself, which propagates negative images of Blacks while at the same time finding something of value in blackness. Negrismo, unlike negritude, generated a dilettante image because of its close similarity to European negrophilia or the scholarly and artistic interest shown in the black by Leo Frobenius ... and others. [23]

One way to see *Cane* is as a series of grotesques—corollaries, in some ways, to Sherwood Anderson's and Waldo Frank's grotesques being published in the same period. This may account in part for the reason that *Cane* was not particularly popular upon its release in 1923. The popular and powerful newspaper reviewer and critic, H. L. Mencken, reviewed both *Holiday* by Waldo Frank and *Dark Laughter* by Sherwood Anderson. *American Mercury* was a new kind of literary "predator" on the market.

The magazine was intended for the intelligent, solvent, urbane American who was skeptical about brummagem utopias and the yearning to save Humanity ... Mencken explained. "Its function is to depict America for the more enlightened sort of Americans—realistically, with good humor and wholly without cant."[24]

The powerful, passionate editor of *American Mercury*, H. L. Mencken, was a major agitating environmental factor between 1921 and 1923, and his opinion of *Holiday* would exercise a critical condemnation of *Cane*.

Frank and Toomer planned to write books about the South (*Holiday* and *Cane*) which would escape the confinements of realism. Unfortunately for Toomer, he was writing in the America of Mencken's Sherwood Anderson. Anderson the realist, not Anderson the experimenter in aesthetic forms, was the one Mencken admired. Although the expatriates in Europe were exploring new avenues of narrative expression which would bear fruit in the future, for the moment it was Mencken's day in court. His judgment of Frank's style in *Holiday* could stand for an indictment of *Cane* as well: "Frank would be improved, I suspect, if he could be set to writing editorials for the New York Times for thirty days and thirty nights." Obviously the "lyrical crystallizations" that revealed character, the oblique plot that set symbols in opposition to one another, and the poetic dialogue—all of which Toomer had admired—made little impression upon the champion of realism.

Of course, *Cane* was not ignored by everyone. The black intellectuals especially recognized Toomer's genius, although they did not quite know what to make of Toomer's book. Few took *Cane* as something to be learned from; or if they did, they always held up a segment or a theme for imitation. For *Opportunity* critic Montgomery Gregory, Toomer was the new Rene Maran, a realistic portrayer of the peasant world of the south; for Langston Hughes, Toomer was both a satirist and a poet; and for Alain Locke, Toomer was primarily a poet and a celebrator of the "folk-spirit" of the race. The black critics all praised him highly (Braithwaite calling him the "morning star" of Negro literature), but the praise was often vague, and they made little attempt to investigate the thematic complexity of *Cane* or—an even more difficult task—its narrative complexity. Although Eric Walrond probably imitated Toomer's elliptical poetical prose style in *Tropic Death* (1926), few in the 1920s, black or white, responded to his exciting use of symbol, myth, and metaphor as ways of giving organic unity to his work and of depicting the South.[25]

Charles Scruggs in *The Sage of Harlem* tells us that Toomer had read Mencken's editorial "Sahara of the Bozart" and recognized his argument for the potential of realism as a liberating literary tool. In fact, Mencken's article deconstructing mythical southern romanticism started a great many people in the South and elsewhere to thinking about its culture and all of its people—particularly African-Americans.

Part of my job in the world is the reading of manuscripts, chiefly by new authors. I go through hundreds every week. This business has taught me some curious things, and among them the fact that the literary passion is segregated geographically, and with it the literary talent. Boston produces better writing than the far West; it is suaver, more careful, finer in detail. Los Angeles leads the whole country in quantity; its weekly output of manuscripts even surpasses that of Greenwich Village. Kansas and Oklahoma are producing capital poets; they tremble on the verge of literature. Chicago leads them all in ideas, originality, vigor; it is the great hatching place of American letters. But the South? The South is almost complete[ly] blank. I don't see one printable manuscript from down there a week. And in my more than three years of steady reading the two Carolinas, Georgia, Alabama, Mississippi, Florida and Tennessee have not offered six taken together.

As for the cause of this practically unanimous sterility I do not profess to be privy to them, but a theory forms and forces itself, and so I pass it on. It is to the following effect: That the civil war actually finished off nearly all the civilized folk in the South and thus left the country to the poor white trash, whose descendents now run it. ... This explains the tragic degeneration of politics in Virginia, and the general cultural decay of such states as Georgia and South Carolina. ...

In such an atmosphere, it must be obvious, the arts cannot flourish.[26]

Here in print, distributed nationally in 1917, was a view of the South that many African-Americans knew to be true. That it was stated by the most powerful Euro-American media voice at the beginning of the century encouraged many of them to write about the real South. Toomer rejected Mencken's position as a literary reviewer on realism (as a pre-eminent literary style and tool) and wrote *Cane*, along with an article titled "The South in Literature," just recently published in *Jean Toomer: Selected Essays and Literary Criticism*, edited by Robert B. Jones.

Scruggs uses a dialogic comparison between novelist and NAACP legend Walter White and Jean Toomer's response to Mencken's advice to young authors to portray the real South as an important element of American literature. Toomer's spiritual orientation made him see the problem differently from Walter White, who clearly could and did pass as a Euro-American, just as Toomer did. White wants to expose the South in *Flight*—that is, help others see what a horrific place it is for African-Americans. Toomer saw the South as a land of great passions that were often dialectically opposed to each other and to the incredible beauty of the landscape itself. In *Cane* he suggests that the struggle can be won only at an individual level first—that African-Americans have to face the truth of their history and potential in the New World and reconcile it with the truth of their history and potential as human beings in the greater world. That historical spiritual confrontation can provide the key for the individual to free him or herself and began to change the culture of the South. Scruggs says, "Since one can never quite understand the South in a rational sense, one can never quite depend on prose (as rational syntactic structure) to reveal the whole truth. Realism is inadequate, because the South isn't quite rational. ... A world as complex as the South needs a complex literary form. It also needs a literary form that avoids the conventional plot format of a beginning, a middle and an end."[27] That would mean, of course, that it would require an analytical literary tool that was expansive enough to see structural and contextual innovation beyond the conventional format of a beginning, a middle, and an end as well.

Toomer wrote an essay, "On Being an American" as did H. L. Mencken. The two essays illuminate two very different processes of accessing Americanness that help the modern reader reexamine their own definitions vis-à-vis American cultural issues. Despite great differences in their views of human beings in general, and African-Americans in particular, they would agree on the necessity of judging men on their merits as individuals. Mencken states in "The Library," May 1931, page 125:

> Personally, I hate to have to think of any man as of a definite race, creed, or color; so few men are really worth knowing that it seems a shameful waste to let an anthropoid prejudice stand in the way of free association with one who is.

This statement is from a man who also said, "The vast majority [of African-Americans in 1926] ... are but two or three inches removed from gorillas: it will be a sheer impossibility, for a long, long while, to interest them in anything above porkchops and boot-leg gin."[28]

Cane attempts to show us the "perceiving subject"—the narrator— who is ideally functioning and evolving as a part of a natal pact between his body, his world, and his self. The narrator experiences a new natural and historical situation and continues to develop as a conscious being throughout the book. Life in *Cane* is like Merleau-Ponty's open notebook, in which we do not yet know what will be written because its form of expression is so original.

> Or it is like a new language; we do not know what works it will accomplish but only that, once it has appeared, it cannot fail to say little or much, to have a history and a meaning. The very productivity or freedom of human life, far from denying our situation, utilizes it and turns it into a means of expression.[29]

This may mean that the reader has to read it more than once and bring his or her real "spirit" to that reading.

A final intersecting current crosses botany with music. Cane or *Saccaharum officinarum-G* or sugar cane is catagorized by herbalogist Scott Cunningham[30] as a feminine plant connected to the planetary power of Venus to effect cycles of love and lust in man and animals. Sugar has long been used as an important element in love and lust potions. Sugar is also scattered to dispel evil and to cleanse and purify areas before rituals and spells. So *Cane* as a literary plant is certainly thematically controlled by love and lust. "The Wind is in the cane, come along" is a call to affection and/or coitus. The phrase embodies the command of something elemental pulling you toward the body of earth to do the things that the earth does. The history of Europe's addiction to sugar (that would lead to their exploitation of the New World) parallels the advent of the Atlantic

Slave Trade and the rise of "Queen Cotton" (another feminine plant with a planetary connection to the moon with the power to effect healing, luck, protection, rain, and fishing magic). Perhaps Toomer's *Cane* is words scattered worldwide to dispel the evil effects of the Atlantic Slave Trade and to cleanse the places and the people who still suffer from its effects. *Cane* can be seen as the beginning of an African-American ritual of cultural cleansing, where all is declared openly and forgiven to move the supplicant to the next stage of illumination, genius, and purity.

This reader views *Cane* holistically as a cyclical poetic drama or a tonal poem with words. Historically, tone poems have been seen strictly as symphonic compositions—for example, those of Richard Strauss and Ottorino Respighi—where the composer experiences a metanoia and in that state of ecstasy writes music of such profound harmonic power that the listener, too, is emotionally "enlightened" and experiences a heightened state of awareness. Symphonic poems or tone poems are judged solely by their ability to reach into our consciousness and create new synaptic pathways that help us see and feel life as a creative and beautiful adventure. Tone poems do not have prescribed structural anomalies and they share very little as common compositions or dynamics. Their difference in form and performance, from established genre prerequisites and from each other, is what creates their ability to impact our consciousness differently within this "wild card" category in symphonic music. Here, I am also applying it to other kinds of musical compositions such as: Freddie Hubbard's "Maiden Voyage," John Lee Hooker's "Back Door Man," Miles Davis's "Time after Time," Nina Simone's "Black Is the Color of My True Love's Hair," Lebo M's "Circle of Life," Sinead O'Connor's "He Moved through the Fair," and John Coltrane's "A Love Supreme." Tone poems are not unlike the haunting line music linking the parts of *Cane*. In this tradition (not the classic definition of Western poetry), *Cane* is a tonal poem of unmatched beauty in the twentieth century. Like readers in the 1920s, contemporary readers can be both amazed and confused by its linguistic registers, adagio gestures, and echoes of the past and present, weaving mystically through its harbinger message of "awake man, awake woman and know your genius."

ST. LOUIS AMERICAN, THURS., APRIL 6, 1978   Page 3

"Cane" To Be Presented At Forest Park College

COMELY LADIES OF "CANE"...*Three female members of the large cast of "Cane" who will be seen at St. Louis Community College at Forest Park April 14-17 are (from left)* **Harriet Walker** *who plays Carrie;* **Sandra Griffin** *whose role is Dorris;* **Gay E. Carraway** *who is Esther in the play which will be directed by* **Chezia Thompson.**

"Cane," a blues novel written by Jean Toomer in 1923, has never been fully understood in literary circles. Chezia Thompson, 26-year-old English Instructor, singer, actress and director, is going to change that. Not only does this multi-talented woman understand Toomer's writing technique, she has adapted and is directing the stage version of "Cane."

The prospect of this brilliant, bold and powerful work of black literature making its stage debut here has generated much excitement around the St. Louis area. "Cane," which deals realistically with race, politics, pain and passion, promises to stir up a mixture of emotions. It will be presented at the Forest Park Community College Performing Arts Center, 5600 Oakland Ave., April 14-17. Performances on April 14, 15 and 17 will be at 8 p.m. and there will be a matinee April 16 at 3 p.m.

Predictions are that "Cane" will be a big hit, but it won't be the first for Thompson who directed "Death Walk," "The Concubines," and "Once Upon A Time In A Garden." Toomer's "Cane" was a contribution and a stimulant to the Harlem Renaissance period. Thompson's contributions may very well mark the beginning of a "St. Louis Renaissance," in the opinion of cast members of "Cane" and other Forest Park dramatic productions.

For more information about "Cane," call 644-9386.

▶ Figure 6.1 Archival Review of *Cane* Performance, April 1978. *St. Louis American*

Illustration by Belynda R. Daniels

Play coming to FPCC

Thompson raises ''Cane''

Jean Toomer's ghost, with a sigh of relief, can finally rest in peace. Thanks go to Chezia Thompson who has adapted and is directing the stage version of "Cane," Toomer's highly controversial novel. Published in 1923, "Cane" is required reading for students in Black Literature classes. The book's literary worth and Toomer's unique style were readily recognized, but opinions are divided concerning "Cane's" content conception. "Cane" therefore, has been dangling in limbo for a definate literature category placement. Instructors, scholars, students and critics in literary circles have argued as to whether "Cane" is a book of poetry, short stories, a collection of bothe or a novel of some sort.

While some have called the book poetically ambiguous, Thompson recognizes "Cane" as an apocalyptic novel in which Toomer exposes the injustice of racial and social stigmas in America, primarily the South. Born in 1894, Toomer reflects through his writing, his intense perceptive ability. He adequately portrays the inner passion, pain and diversity of other Afro-Americans with his tyle of word expression. According to Thompson, Toomer's style has been misunderstoc, because in "Cane," he uses the "Vertical Technique" of writing.

"Cane" which deals realistically with race, politics and passion promises to stir up a mixture of emotions. It will be performed at the Forest Park Community College Performing Arts Center from April 14—17. Predictions are that "Cane" will be a hit, but it won't be the first for Thompson who also directed "Death Walk," "The Concubines," and "Once Upon a Time In a Garden." Toomer's ghost will be tickled to life that his novel has finally fallen into the right hands.

Gladys A. Coggswell

▶ Figure 6.2 Archival Review of *Cane* Performance, April 1978. St. Louis Community College at Forest Park Communication Department publication called "The Scene"

CHEZIA THOMPSON REVIVES "CANE"

By Gladys Coggswell

Jean Toomer's ghost, with a sigh of relief, can finally rest in peace, thanks to Chezia Thompson. Thompson, a multi-talented 26 year old Virgo, is an English Composition and Ritual Drama Instructor at Forest Park Community College. She has adapted and is directing the stage version of "Cane", Toomer's highly controversial novel.

Thompson who holds a bachelor s degree in English and Black Literature, and a masters degree in Curriculum Organizing and Comparative Literature, both from Washington University. The recipient of the Aviation Systems Command Merit Service Award, Paul Robeson Black Artist Award, and several other honors, Thompson was inducted into Who's Who in American Colleges and Universities; 1972-73.

Not one to do things half way, Thompson, while earning her bachelors degree, took the time to do extensive literary research. Going directly to the source, Thompson researched African Literature at the University of Africa in Lagos, Nigeria, and Caribbean Literature at the University of the West Indies in Mona and at the Haitia—American Institute in Port-au-Prince, Haiti.

Chezia Thompson as "Avey" in the stage version of "Cane".

Though constantly in pursuit of intellectualism and perfection, an intriguing parodox is Thompson's profound belief in esoteric philosophy. She has been labeled a "genious", "witch", "mystic" and "Prophet". Whatever she is, according to members in the cast of "Cane", Thompson generates an exhuberant energy which is highly contagious. One member of the cast remarked, "she makes us feel as if we can accomplish anything or play any part that we attempt."

Published in 1923, "Cane" is required reading for students in Black Literature Classes. The book's literary worth and Toomer's unique style of "Cane's'' content. The book therefore, has been dangling in limbo for a definate literature category placement. Instructor's, scholars, students and critics in literary circles have argued as to whether "Cane" is a book of poetry, short stories, a collection of both or a novel of some sort.

While some have called "Cane" poetically, ambiguous, Thompson recognizes "Cane" as an apolcalyptic novel in which Toomer exposes the injustice of racial and social stigmas in America, primarily the South. Born in 1894, Toomer reflects through his writing, an intense perceptive ability. He adequately portrays the inner passion, pain and diversity of other Afro Americans with his style of word expression. According to Thompson, Toomer's style has been misunderstood because in "Cane", he uses the "vertical technique" of writing.

Thompson discovered the existence of this technique while researching literature in Africa and the West Indies. "It's a cyclic form of expression which has developed by the Negritude Writers" says Thompson. These writers, Chicaya U' Tamsa, (Congolese) Aime Ceasaire and Leon Damas both from the West Indies formulated the philosophy of the Negritude movement in the early twentieth century

and the "verticle technique" was employed as a vehicle to awaken and promote Black Consciousness. These writers have also been accredited with encouraging the birth of the Harlem Renaissance. It was during this time that Toomer was inspired to write.

"Cane" which deals realistically with race, politics, pain and passion promises to stir up a mixture of emotions. It will be performed at Forest Park Community College in the Performing Arts Center auditorium from April 14-17. Predictions are that "Cane" will be a hit, but it won't be the first for Thompson who also directed "Death Walk", "The Concubines", and "Once Upon A Time In A Garden". Jean Toomer's ghost just might be tickled to life that "Cane" has finally fallen into the right hands.

Continued from Page 18.

as I could reach. The character of the citizen's who have already rallied to my support has given me confidence."

Another reason for Mr. Goins' confidence was the acceptance, by Dr. Jerome Williams, of the Goins for Congress Committee Chairmanship. Dr. Williams has said, "I accepted the position because I believe that Mr. Goins is honest, capable, and has integrity. He has proven his astuteness and his ability by the tremendous service he has rendered to the City as License Collector and as Sheriff." Mr. Goins responded with great satisfaction stating, "This expression of confidence gives my campaign just the right kind of kick-off. To have a man of the stature, ability and dedication of Dr. Jerome Williams to chair the efforts of the many outstanding citizens who are rallying behind my Candidacy assures that we will have guidance of proven ability and outstanding character."

▶ Figure 6.3 Archival Review of *Cane* Performance, April 1978. *Kingsway Magazine.*

St. Louis Community College at Forest Park Speech/Theatre Department
presents

CANE

Adapted and Directed by *Chezia Thompson*
Sets and Lighting by *Vance Fulkerson*
Fight Choreography by *John L. Brown*
Original Musical Arrangements by *Gladys Coggswell*
Slide Photography by *David Francsico*

The Cast

Karintha I	*Emily Diane Hockaday*
Karintha II	*Lisa Dabney*
Becky	*Shirley Phillips*
The Earth	*Gladys Coggswell*
Carma	*Randy Allisia Page*
Fern	*Debra Craig*
Ester	*Gay E. Carraway*
Louisa	*Harriet Rose Walker*
Avey	*Chezia Thompson*
Dorris	*Sandra Griffin*
The Celestials	*Bertha Thompson*
	Claudine James Thompson
	Melanie D. Selvey
	Ouida Bryant
Murial	*Elizabeth A. Watkins*
Mrs. Pribby	*Thelma Cahill*
Bona	*Sue Jordan*
Helen	*Mary Beutler*
Mame	*Bertha Thompson*
Cora	*Harriet Rose Walker*
Carrie K.	*Claudine Jame Thompson*
Stella	*Marilyn Wilson*
Little Girls	*Djuana Garrett*
	Awrey Garrett
	La Tonja Thomas
	Tracey Parks
	Princess Hughes
White Woman I	*Mary Beutler*
White Woman II	*Cathy Mock*
Young Black Man	*Boule Rashid*
Lewis	*Michael Bonds*
Ole Black Man	*John Durham*
Ralph Kabnis	*Carl Chamberlain*
John Stone / The Sheriff	*Steve Bolhafre*
Barlo / Doorman	*James H. Thompson*
Bane / Ned / Dan Moore	*Clyde Hitchens*
Doc / John	*Gary Lunceford*
Art	*Steve Bolhafre*
Fred Halsey	*John Durham*
Young Boys	*Truman Cogswell, Jr.*
	Timothy Ferguson
Tom Burwell / Professor Layman	*Everett Marshall*
Bob Stone	*Michael Schrader*
Hanby	*Ivory Roach*
Father John	*Ivory Roach*
Accompanists	*Marsha Washington Upchurch*
	Randy A. Page

▶ **Figure 6.4 Original Production Program**

Synopsis

TIME: 1923

I. Place – The South, the countryside in Georgia
   Cycle One – The Incursion
     Karintha
     Becky
     Carma
   Cycle Two – The Atrophy
     Fern
II. Place – The South, small town's mainstreet in Georgia
     Ester
   Cycle Three – The Destruction
     Louisa

INTERMISSION

III. Place – The North, Washington D.C. – Seventh Street & Chicago
     Avey
     Dorris
     Muriel
     Bona
   Cycle Four – The Rejuvenation
IV. Place – The South, small town's mainstreet in Georgia – Kabnis' Room,
   The Parlor of Fred Halsey, Fred Halsey's Workshop
     Ralph Kabnis

Production Staff

Assistants to the Director	Lisa Dabney
	Karen Buckner
Dance Supervisor	Bertha Thompson
Staff Shop Foreman	Al McFarland
Student Shop Foreman	Ken Yorgan
Projections	Karen Buckner
Spot Lights	Alonze Nsoah
	Gary Robertson
Stage Manager	Karen Buckner
Floor Manager	Shirley Phillips
Set Construction	Jerry French, Ken Yorgan
	Al McFarland, Morris Singfield,
	Gary Robertson, Shirley Phillips,
	Herald Lee, Cathy Mock, Vladez Darris,
	Dan Mestris
Prop Mistress	Tracey Parks
Publicity	Sylvia Dabney, Carol Jean Handley-Marley
	Gladys Coggswell, Carl Chamberlain
Light Board	Jerry French, Morris Singfield
Sound Board	Dennis Mestris
Costumes	Alice in Parafunally in Maryland Plaza
House Manager	Richard Salamon

EPIPHANY

EPIPHANY
Toward a Unifying Theory

WHAT'S IN A NAME?

Eugene Pinchback was stripped of half of his true name at birth.

He reclaimed it as a young adult in the form of Eugene Toomer and then changed it to fit the new self that he was forging as Jean Toomer. Notice the inherent ambiguities of the name in regards to gender and ethnicity. The name Jean Toomer tells you nothing about the person as opposed to Eugene—identifiably male—and Pinchback—historically recognizable. Toomer's process embodies the wisdom of an old Negro spiritual titled "I Told Jesus It Would Be All Right If He Changed My Name." Historically, Africans enslaved in the New World (e.g., in the case of the *Amistad* Revolt) had their names changed against their will as a part of the strategy to enslave them. The spiritual suggests that Africans believed the process worked in reverse: that you could choose to name yourself as the part of your strategy to free yourself from slavery. Hence, the Negro spiritual "Hush, Hush, Somebody's Callin Ma Name" incorporates the concept of recognizing the power of your true name, when it is pronounced as an announcement. (Examples include: Sojourner Truth, Olaudah Equiano, Frederick Douglass, and so on.)

In a metalinguistic sense, changing one's name transforms one's sign and symbol power; that is, it transforms one's identity either into an enigma or into a discernible force. (One example is the American preoccupation with acquiring academic degrees as a way of changing one's name.) With all of the name changing and even with having lived through three traumatic evolutionary leaps in the history of America (World War I, the advent of *Sputnik,* and the Black Revolution of the 1960s), Jean

Toomer was only able to reconcile the dualities of his multiple ethnic heritage by selecting an environment that allowed him to actualize the broadest possible definition of his humanity within American society. He joined the Quakers.

Toomer's America did not allow him to accept the dualities of his heritage. The simple dialectic that controls former Senate majority leader Trent Lott's America today still defines how race (as a nonscientific delineation of *homo sapiens*) split numerous Africans in the New World at visual, psychological, political, and economic levels. The various periods of Toomer's delicate mental health attest to the problem of his racial-cultural schizophrenia and suggest a possible rationale for the increased incidence of mental illness and suicide among African-Americans today.

Not only writers, but many African-American artists have had similar difficulties in resolving the problem of their racial-cultural dilemma. However, if the truth about the evolution of European culture (in relationship to the technological and cultural societies in Africa that preceded it) were taught, African-Americans would know that much of what they are resisting has very little to do with being "white-skinned" or of "pure" European genetic origin. It is a problem because it clouds the basic truth that Toomer discovered before Franz Boas's research: Despite the rationalization of historic acts toward peoples of color, the result is Toomer's vision of Americans as a unique blend of all the elements of humankind.

Toomer, like contemporary African-Americans, shares similar problems and similar cultural–aesthetic dispositions about many things with many descendants of other Africans throughout the African diaspora. *Cane* remains one of the best assessments and depictions of the power of African-American culture. *Cane* remains the sentinel standing at the beginning of the twentieth century decrying the horror of slavery and segregation and exalting the beauty of the culture and the people who emerged from it, in a voice that is both ancient and modern.

While *Cane* is not directly biographical, it reveals life-changing events and people in Toomer's life in ways that make its structure more uniquely fitted to chronicle the stages of acculturation of Africans in the New World. As a dynamic sociological process, acculturation demonstrates movement into or toward the mainstream of society's capital and power-holding group. There are different strata of competing systems of meanings that create overlapping physiological and psychological tensions at both the real and literary level. From the kind of "November Cotton Flower" beauty of Toomer's mother, to the ambivalence of Toomer (as Paul) in a Chicago college in "Bona and Paul"; from the omniscient third-person voice of the narrator in the beginning who becomes a first-person narrating voice with a name, *Cane* reveals the dialectic of the twentieth century to us. It also hints at the beginning of an African-American literature which is not rooted in the victimization of the American slave narrative, but in the artistic innovation of written and oral African literature extending back in time for centuries.

This study utilizes several relevant models from African literature to suggest an understanding of Toomer's way of handling language and the use of the "moon phases drawings" announcing the text. The double nomenclature of Toomer's real identity and Toomer's predominant male voice changing shape and nuance in *Cane* is what drives the calm hysteria of the text. A double consciousness inherited from the previous century is what drives the twenty-first-century American reader of *Cane*. The dilemma of such celebrities as songstress Mariah Carey or golf genius Tiger Woods means that W. E. B. Du Bois's pronouncement of the color line as the greatest problem continues in the twenty-first century.

The foci of this inquiry into the structure and themes of *Cane* have been designed as a tool to use in the classroom. They are reducible to three concerns: (1) What is *Cane*'s African-American quality? (2) What is *Cane*'s literary quality? and (3) What is *Cane*'s American quality? More important, the study suggests a strategy for teaching *Cane* that encourages students to grapple with these questions in an effort to gain a clearer understanding of how literature functions as a mirror of social behavior. The intent is to create a medium for the reader of *Cane* to see the relationship between reading American literary works and understanding their relevance to the study of American culture and history and the impact they have on the reader's life.

Reviewing the lives of *Cane*'s Americans in the classroom can help students see literature from a different point of view. Written African-American literature has evolved out of a tradition of oral literature, whose purpose is to manifest the power of words. The worldview that dictates this tradition in John Mbiti's *The Mind of Africa* designates the cooperative, balancing forces in the universe as the power of Man (Muntu), the power of God (Kuntu), the power of things (Kintu), and the power of time and place (Hantu). The power of words is to effect transformation. Literature was initially simply important words spoken in celebration, remembrance, and/or commemoration. Historically, literature has been a powerful critical tool in developing human potential.

Ogotemmeli, as the master Dogon philosopher in Marcel Griaule's *Conversations with Ogotemmeli: An Introduction to Dogon Religious Ideas*, explains the power of words as Nummo—the second entity to be born in our earthly universe. Nummo was given the conceptual understanding of this universe by primeval powers before the creation of humankind. It was Nummo who related critical survival strategies to the humans attempting to build a civilization in Dogon society. The language construct of Nummo is both poetic and metaphysical while simultaneously being situated within the real world. For the reader, *Cane* represents the power of Nummo within the realities of 1923 America. Aside from its value as an intellectual lesson in literary analysis, teaching it will also help students trying to develop personal and broader social strategies to eliminate racism and sexism in the twenty-first century.

THE AMERICAN LITERARY MAINSTREAM'S RESPONSE TO *CANE* IN 1923

Cane is fragmentary. In this medley of poems, sketches and short stories, Frank—for is not "Jean Toomer" a polite fiction?—exhibits the methods of his workshop rather than his finished product. (By the way, we here assume the attitude of a certain critic in the present Rembrandt controversy who said, "What does it matter whether Rembrandt painted those pictures or Bols, so long as they are genuine Rembrandts!") But as many prefer Rembrandt's pen scratchings on bits of paper, to his paintings, so some readers will find even greater beauty and more truth in these fragments from the emotional life of colored folk picked up at random in the streets of a little Georgia town, of Washington and of Chicago.[1]

An anonymous review in *The Springfield Republican* also focuses on *Cane*'s fragmentary style. *The Boston Transcript* review expresses a dangerously misleading concept that was perhaps held widely but not often repeated to Toomer verbally or in print media—that being African-American had some inherent connection to being "mournful, loving beauty, ignorant, full of passion, untutored and entirely unconnected with the brain." This stereotypical image was held by many Euro-Americans in the early 1900s, and a superficial reading of *Cane* may seem to support the image of the ignorant, uneducated, singing, praying, mystified "darkie in ole massa's souf" in the twentieth century.

On the other hand, the African-Americans in *Cane*, except Lewis (in "Kabnis"), are not a threat to segregation in American society. That they appear not to have the slightest chance of affecting the American socio-political system must have been very comforting to many Euro-Americans reading *Cane* or a review of it. Unlike its predecessors, *Souls of Black Folk* and *The Autobiography of an Ex-Colored Man*, *Cane* was a non-aggressive portrayal of black people wrestling unsuccessfully with the legacy of slavery in the modern world. *Cane*'s characters did not encroach upon the world of the Euro-American urbanite. On the contrary, they were neoslaves and seemed to be doomed to remain "in their places" in the American South or ineffective and disoriented in the North. If the African-American sons of southern blue bloods were the only problems American literature and society had, they and civilization were safe. Ralph Kabnis was a "sensible character" in the American literary tradition. He represented the dilemma of the tragic mulatto played out again, and since the mulatto was a "creature" apart from the Negro, he could be reckoned with differently. However, the New Negro was born out of the fury of Kabnis's darker-skinned brother, who did not want to occupy his assigned "darker" place in society or give up being African-American. The protagonist in Richard Wright's *Native Son,* for example, is not a "sensible character" in the mainstream American literary tradition. There are no "sensible" answers for his dilemma as a poverty-stricken African-American in an urban setting.

Even Toomer's mentor and friend, novelist Sherwood Anderson, is revealed by Mark Helbling[2] in "Sherwood Anderson and Jean Toomer" to be more of a subtle racist than anyone would expect. Helbling insists that Anderson harbored his own reasons for identifying with Toomer's artistry in *Cane.* Anderson refused to support the concept of progressive Negro Art by casually dismissing the whole question of its existence in an article for Alain Locke. Helbling writes, "Anderson's perception of the Black as a primitive figure has roots deep in the cultural experience of America."[3] It is Anderson's own psychic disharmony that led him to identify with the Black American, for he perceived the Black man to be a kind of natural craftsman whose very existence was itself a form of art." Helbling's analysis makes Anderson's perception of *Cane* and Toomer's position on his analyis much clearer and much less romantic.

Anderson's reading of *Cane* may be one of the reasons its form received more attention than its themes. It may also explain why neither Euro-American nor African-American people found it alarmingly militant or politically threatening. Robert Littell in "A Review of *Cane*" is careful to focus on the themes and not the structure. He points out that there is more to Toomer's vision than meets the eye initially. He says explicitly that *Cane* is not the South of the

> ... chivalrous gentleman, the fair lady, the friendly decaying mansion, of mammie, cotton and pickaninnies ... *Cane* does not remotely resemble any of the familiar, superficial views of the South on which we have been brought up on. On the contrary, Mr. Toomer's view is more than the account of things seen by a novelist—lyric, symbolic, oblique, seldom actual.[4]

Toomer's understanding of the mainstream Euro-American aesthetic enabled him to speak to its artists in a "sensible recognizable voice." For instance, Victor Kramer in "The Mid-Kingdom of Crane's 'Black Tambourine' and Toomer's *Cane*"[5] says that the similarities between the two works are too striking to be coincidental. Kramer establishes the fact that Crane and Toomer were friends with mutual mentors, Waldo Frank and Gorham Munson, which gives the works an informal link. The preoccupation of both works is that black culture must span the gap between past and present. Crane and Toomer each perceived the condition of the African-American man as that of someone in a dark hole yet confronted by the closed door of society. Toomer saw the strength and power of an agrarian culture slowly being eaten away by urbanization and industrialization. (The Agrarian Literary Movement by southern Euro-American writers would come in part as response to H. L. Mencken's widespread press criticism of southern culture and literature.) American society promised privilege but continued to relegate African-Americans to the role of menial. *Cane* and "Black Tambourine" both stress how many African-Americans sustain themselves despite the inequities in their environment.

Kramer compares the poetic figure (sitting in a darkened room with a tambourine on the wall) in "Black Tambourine" to the old Negro beggar Dan Moore meets on the streets of Washington, D.C. (in "Box Seat"), and to Father John, whom Kabnis meets in the cellar of Fred Halsey's house in Georgia in "Kabnis." In the Crane poem, a roach is a metaphor for the alienated black person, who attempts to bridge a gap to modern society. In *Cane*, Kabnis insults Hanby by calling him a cockroach and insults Father John in the same manner. For Kramer, the cockroach image links Toomer's work to Crane's.

In a final analysis, Clifford Mason's vision of Toomer provides one of the most penetrating views of *Cane*.

> But his [Toomer's] people were more than bucolic specimens who had that peasant stability that gives so much dignity to the rural life. They were also the children of an urban enlightenment who had their desires for more than their world could offer but who understood all the beauty that it held. They were disillusioned, neurotic and tragically oppressed people. They were profound, enduring, searching people, who fashioned their self-truth out of a chaos that was not of their own making. Toomer, in his realization that a race cannot stand for anything it has not lived within the dynamic of its own sub-consciousness, took every stripe of the Black, southern original and kneaded him into his artistic whole. . . .
>
> When Toomer talked about the new slope of consciousness and the superior logic of the metaphor, he was talking about a controlled mysticism, a rare memory fused sense of perception that surpasses all concepts of the physical science and of tangible reality. The definition of what one man can feel and yet not artic-

ulate, know and not be able to transmit, experience and yet not understand—
these are the effects that he creates with his sweep of poetry-prose, his shifting
scenes and seemingly innumerable characters foaled in as disparate a set of
places and circumstances as are imaginable, and yet all tied back to that Georgia
dirt—colored red from black blood.[6]

Cane cannot be easily categorized into a specific historical genre.
There is the fact of Toomer's ordering the logic of *Cane* before sending it
to the publisher with the marked cycle phases that were originally elimi-
nated for the early publications.

This study calls those arcs "moon phases," which probably reflects
what Toomer saw in the sky while writing *Cane*. They are time markers,
oracular guides for the reader. These arcs represent an ascending moon,
a moon at complete moonrise, and a descending moon, dividing *Cane*
into three original sections: The first arc comes before "Karintha," the second before "Seventh Street," and the third before "Kabnis." We know that
the structure is intentional—not accidental. In 1921, Toomer was working with a vision of Americans and American literature that America is still
trying to actualize today. So whether labeled "the cyclic novel" or the psychological drama/novel, *Cane* would remain a haunting enigma.
Nevertheless, by examining how *Cane* functions structurally, the reader
can describe what it is and what it does with some accuracy. That task
requires new tools of literary analysis that make *Cane* comprehensible at
an elemental level for the reader—the ultimate goal of this study. *Cane*'s
thematic and structural unity lies in its ability to focus on and magnify a
sufficiently broad and objective view of the impact of racism on the ordi-
nary American citizen, without using capitalist or Marxist rhetoric.
Moreover, the theme and structure of *Cane* are most clearly seen through
the Vertical Technique as a unique way of employing images in both fiction and poetry to create a new assembled aesthetic: that is, none of the
parts are greater than the whole—and the whole cannot exist without all
of the parts which are uniquely nonreplicable. *Cane* offers readers a lesson in the complexities of caste, class, color, and the impact of American
democracy on a collision course with racism in the early twentieth
century.

In *Singers of Daybreak*, Houston Baker says that *Cane* reveals Toomer
as "a writer of genius and the book itself as a protest novel, a portrait of
the artist, and a thorough delineation of the Black situation."[7] Although
this study refers to *Cane* as a poetic drama, labeling its genre is ultimately
not as important as discovering a way to explain its design comprehensi-
bly. Using the Vertical Technique and Blues Motif as analytical tools, this
study attempts to reveal *Cane* as a coherent, unified dramatic work that

can be taught easily in the classroom setting. The photographs of the first and only complete staging of *Cane* accompany this text as an instructional aid.

It is impossible to determine the exact name of the new literary form *Cane* represented on its release in 1923; but discovering how its structure works is critically important in deciphering its meaning at macroanalytical and microanalytical levels. Toomer's comment on the matter of labeling has provided both a warning and a guide in my attempt.

> They can pile up records and labels a mile high, and in the end they will find, pinned under that pile not me but their own intelligence.[8]

APPENDIX

The Poetic Essay Form: An Alternative Writing Invention

The intense study of *Cane* can be greatly enhanced by a pedagogical strategy known as the Reader Response Theory. This model can provide the link between developing reading and analytical ability, audience sensitivity, and versatility as a writer that can foster the more broad-based cultural orientation necessary for succeeding in today's and tomorrow's information-driven society. A structural diagram of the theory resembles Figure A.1.

Toomer offers the challenge of innovation in his writing; as a corollary, I offer you the challenge of being innovative in your writing about his work. I want to suggest a different format for you to engage your structural creativity as an analytical tool in writing first about *Cane* and then other things. Try it and email me about what happens and how you feel about your writing: drcbt@verizon.net.

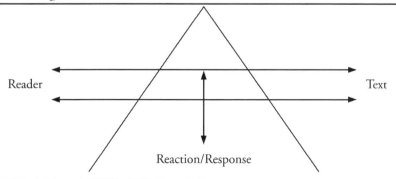

▶ Figure A.1 Reader Response Model

THE POETIC ESSAY

Like the cyclical poetic drama or tone poem, the poetic essay engages a different process to create an analytical essay. The change in process and structure almost always produces a change in logic—that is, the conventional relationship between ideas may take unconventional turns but ultimately should aim to impact the consciousness of the reader.

Prologue—Section One

Disregard the conventional concept of an introduction (for a general audience) as an overview of what you are about to discuss in your essay. Instead, identify who or what organization or group to which you are writing. Write a statement detailing how you first encountered the subject: under what conditions and to what end; why the exploration of the subject is or is not important to you. Write it in your first-person voice and be very specific in what detail you use to support your statement. Be descriptive in this statement—help the reader understand your point of entry into the subject of your essay. Use a point in your personal, professional, geographical, political, and/or ethnic group history to "center" the focus on your specific subject. Don't inhibit your creativity by assigning yourself a certain number of paragraphs. Just write at this point. If you want to, you can edit it to be shorter later.

Contact—Section Two

In this second section of your paper, write a statement describing obvious "truths" about the subject. Your assessment should include objective physical historical facts delineating a primary view of what is generally understood about your subject. Connect your related facts with your reason for writing about this subject. Write several lines in support of your reason for the subject's importance or lack thereof. Don't try to summarize your position on all known facts about your subject. Choose only the elements that matter to how you see the world and your place in it.

Engagement—Section Three

Decide on at least four points that you want the reader to understand about your subject. Carefully word each point and explain it in as much detail as possible, using factual data and your perception of the factual data. Work on each point separately, developing your explanation as fully as possible. Explain what the four points have in common, so that the reader is not trying to guess his or her way through your worldview's epistemology.

Epiphany—Section Four

Write a statement about what you (the writer) learned from your current exploration of the subject. Explain to the reader how you learned it, what your process was, and what importance it has or lacks. Write a final sentence or statement on what you hope the reader will understand from what you've written about your selected topic. Then stop writing and review what you have already written. Revise and edit on sentence and paragraph levels until you reach your final typed, formatted edit. Don't be afraid to try new syntactical structures, but always ask the question: "How can I make sure that this will make sense to the reader?" Give the final typed and edited version to someone who is included in your target reader audience. Ask them to read it and write comments, editorial suggestions, or corrections on it. Review what your reader says and make your final decisions about what to change before printing your final edited copy.

NOTES

CHAPTER ONE

1. Jean Toomer, *Cane*, Introduction by Darwin Turner (New York: Liveright, 1975), 2.
2. Toomer, *Cane*, 5.
3. Toomer, *Cane*, 10-11.
4. Toomer, *Cane*, 20-25.
5. Toomer, *Cane*, 26.
6. Toomer, *Cane*, 27.
7. Toomer, *Cane*, 28-35.
8. Toomer, *Cane*, 28-35.
9. Toomer, *Cane*, 45-47.
10. Toomer, *Cane*, 49.
11. Toomer, *Cane*, 50-53.
12. Toomer, *Cane*, 53.
13. Toomer, *Cane*, 56-57.
14. Toomer, *Cane*, 68.
15. Toomer, *Cane*, 69.
16. Toomer, *Cane*, 78.
17. Toomer, *Cane*, 106-116.

CHAPTER TWO

1. P. Chike Onwauchi, "Negritude in Perspective," *Black World* (October 1971), 4-6.
2. K. Curtis Lyle, *Drunk on God* (New York: Diamond Duck and Joe Death Press, 1980). K. Curtis Lyle, *15 Predestination Weather Reports (Beyond Baroque)* (New York: Diamond Duck and Joe Death Press, 1981).
3. Bonnie J. Barthold, *Black Time: Fiction of African, the Caribbean and the United States* (New Haven: Yale University Press, 1981), 7.
4. Barthold, *Black Time: Fiction of African, the Caribbean and the United States*, 9-10.
5. Barthold, *Black Time: Fiction of Africa, the Caribbean and the United States*, 18.

6. Houston A. Baker, Jr., *Singers of Daybreak: Studies in Black American Literature,* (Washington, D.C.: Howard University Press, 1983), 57.

7. Baker, *Singers of Daybreak,* 62.

8. Chezia Thompson, "Transfiguration: The African Woman in Traditional and Modern Society," *Proud Magazine* 6, No. 2 (March/April 1975), 18-19.

9. Toomer, *Cane,* 10.

10. Charles Davis, "Jean Toomer and the South: Region and Race as Elements within a Literary Imagination," *Studies in the Literary Imagination,* VII, No. 2 (Fall 1974), 30-31.

11. Chris Antoinides, *Jean Toomer: The Burden of Impotent Pain,* Pt. A US ISSN 0419-4209, Pt. B US ISSN 0419-4217, Ann Arbor, Michigan, 1976.

12. Hargis Westerfield, "Jean Toomer's Fern: A Mythical Dimension," *College Language Association Journal,* 14, No. 3 (March 1971), 274.

13. Bernard Bell, "A Key to the Poems in *Cane,*" *College Language Association Journal,* 14, No. 3 (March 1971), 253.

14. Edward E. Waldron, "The Search for Identity in Jean Toomer's Esther," *College Language Association Journal,* XIV, No. 3 (March 1971), 277-280.

15. Robert Bone, *The Negro Novel in America* (New Haven: Yale University Press, 1965).

16. Odette C. Martin, "Cane: Method and Myth," *Obsidian: Black Literature in Review,* Vol. 2, No. 1 (Spring 1976), 9-10.

17. Bernard Bell in "A Key to the Poems in *Cane*" says, "The grim image of a woman in 'Portrait in Georgia' forcefully establishes the sexual link between the Southern ritual of lynching and the myths of white purity and black bestiality" (257).

18. Rafael A. Cancel, "Male and Female Interrelations in Toomer's *Cane,*" *Negro American Literature,* Vol. 5, No. 1 (Spring 1971), 27.

19. Patricia Chase, "The Women in *Cane,*" *College Language Association Journal,* XIV, No.3 (March 1971), 267.

20. Louise Blackwell, "Jean Toomer's *Cane* and Biblical Myth," *College Language Association Journal,* Vol. XVII, No. 4 (June 1974), 539.

21. Bernard Bell, "Portrait of the Artist as the High Priest of Soul," *Black World,* XXIII, No. 11 (September 1974), 12-13.

22. George Kopf, "The Tensions in Jean Toomer's Theater," *College Language Association,* XVII, No. 4 (June 1974), 498.

23. Elizabeth Schultz, "Jean Toomer's 'Box Seat': The Possibility for 'Constructive Crisis,'" *Black American Literature Forum,* Vol. 13, No. 1 (Spring 1979), 7.

24. See the portrayal of "The Nothing" in the film *The Never-Ending Story.*

25. B. P. Grimaud, *The Great Etteilla of the Egyptian Tarot* (Nancy-France: J. N. Simon, 1969), Card 17.

26. Jack M. Christ, "Jean Toomer's 'Bona and Paul': The Innocence and the Artifice of Words," *Negro American Literature Forum,* Vol. 9, No. 2 (Summer 1975), 45.

27. Michael Krasny, "The Aesthetic Structure of Jean Toomer's *Cane,*" *Negro American Literature Forum,* 4, No. 2 (Summer 1975), 42.

28. Alice Poindexter Fisher, "The Influence of Ouspensky's Tertium Organum upon Jean Toomer's *Cane,*" *College Language Association Journal,* XVII, No. 4 (June 1974), 508.

CHAPTER THREE

1. P. Chike Onwauchi, "Negritude in Perspective," *Black World* (October 1971), 4-6.
2. Frances Cress Welsing, M.D., *The Cress Theory of Color Confrontation and Racism-White Supremacy* (Washington, D.C.: C. R. Publisher, 1970).
3. Boubacar Barry, "Afro-Americans and Futa Djalon," *Global Dimensions of the African Diaspora*, edited by Joseph E. Harris (Washington, D.C.: Howard University Press, 1982).
4. Edward Brathwaite, "Race and the Divided Self," *Black World* (July 1972), 55-56.
5. Barry, "Afro-Americans and Futa Djalon," 283.
6. Aimé Césaire, *Return to My Native Land,* Paris: Presence Africaine, 1968, 54-55.
7. John Reed, Clive Wake, trans. *Translation from the Night: Selected Poems by Jean-Joseph Rabearivelo* (London: Heinemann, 1975) 49.
8. Césaire, *Return to My Native Land,* 41-43.

CHAPTER FOUR

1. Jason Berry, "Jazz Literature," *Southern Exposure,* Vol. VI, No. 3 (Fall 1978), 43.
2. Bruce Cook, *Listen to the Blues* (New York: Charles Scribner's Sons, 1973).
3. Cook, *Listen to the Blues,* 24-25.
4. J. H. Pelham, *P. G. M.* (Hannibal, Missouri: Journal Printing Company, 1905), 90-91.
5. W. W. Long, C. B. Thompson, "Blues as the Facts of Life," *Mississippi Delta Blues Festival 1980* (Greenville, Mississippi: Mississippi Action for Community Education, Inc., 1980), 2.
6. Cook, *Listen to the Blues,* 26.
7. Samuel B. Charters, *The Bluesmen* (New York: Oak Publications, 1967).
8. Leonard Goines, "The Blues as Black Therapy," *Black World* (November 1973), 35.
9. Daphne Duval Harrison, "The Blues from the Black Woman's Perspective," *Sagala: A Journal of Art and Ideas,* No. 3 (1983), 21.
10. Stephen E. Henderson, "Blues Poetry and Poetry of the Blues Aesthetic: A Study of Craft and Tradition," *Sagala: A Journal of Art and Ideas,* No. 3 (1983).
11. Ralph Ellison, "Richard Wright's Blues," *Shadow and Act* (New York: A Signet Book, 1964), 90.
12. Gene Bluestein, "The Blues as a Literary Theme," *The Massachusetts Review* (Autumn 1967), 609.
13. Alice Walker, *In Search of Our Mothers' Gardens: Womanist Prose* (New York: Harcourt, Brace and Jovanovich, 1983), 231-233.
14. Benjamin F. McKeever, "Cane as Blues," *Negro American Literature Forum,* 4, No. 2 (July 1970), 61.
15. Arnold B. Rhodes, *The Mighty Acts of God* (Atlanta: John Knox Press, 1964) 53, 79.
16. Zolar, *The Encyclopedia of Ancient and Forbidden Knowledge* (New York: Popular Library, 1970), 438.
17. P. R. Stephensen and Israel Regardie, *The Legend of Aleister Crowley* (Saint Paul, Minnesota: Llewellyn Publications, 1970), 24.
18. G. H. Bass, "Sinnerman" on Nina Simone's *Pastel Blues* PHS 600-187 (Chicago: Philips Records/A Division of Mercury Record Corporations), N.D.
19. E. B. Marks Corp., "Strange Fruit" on Nina Simone's *Pastel Blues* PHS 600-187.
20. William Ferris, *Blues from the Delta* (Garden City: Doubleday, 1978).

21. Gil Scott-Heron and Brian Jackson, *It's Your World* (New York: Arista Records, Inc., 1976).

22. G. H. Bass, "See-Line Woman" on Nina Simone—Broadway-blues-ballads PHS-600-148 (Philips Records/A Division of Mercury Record Productions, Inc.), N.D.

23. Benjamin F. McKeever, "Cane as Blues," *Negro American Literature Forum*, Vol. 4, No. 2 (July 1970), 63.

24. Ronald Dorris, "Jean Toomer's 'Kabnis': Family Portrait as Face of the South," *Network 2000: In Spirit of the Harlem Renaissance*, Volume 12 (2004), 17-20.

CHAPTER FIVE

1. Jean Toomer, "Earth-Being," *The Wayward and the Seeking: A Collection of Writings by Jean Toomer*, edited by Darwin Turner (Washington, D.C.: Howard University Press, 1982), 23.

2. Toomer, "Earth-Being," 24-25.

3. Toomer, "Incredible Journey," 32-33.

4. Jean Toomer, "On Being an American," *The Wayward and the Seeking: A Collection of Writings by Jean Toomer*, edited by Darwin Turner (Washington, D.C.: Howard University Press, 1982), 33.

5. Charles T. Davis, "Jean Toomer and the South: Region and Race as Elements within a Literary Imagination," *Studies in the Literary Imagination*, VII, No. 2 (Fall 1974), 23-38.

6. Clyde Taylor, "The Second Coming of Jean Toomer," *Obsidian: Black Literature in Review*, Vol. 1, Issue 3 (1975), 57.

7. Toomer, "Earth-Being," 53-54.

8. Toomer, "Earth-Being," 6. Turner says in his editorial notes for "On Being an American" that Toomer's grandmother was not fond of black men, but neither he nor she took the prejudice seriously. Other members of the family supposedly had no prejudice. Race and color were rarely mentioned.

9. Toomer, "Earth-Being," 74-75.

10. Per M. Bergman and Mort N. Bergman, *The Chronological History of the Negro in America* (New York: The New American Library, 1969), 364.

11. Minority Americans have a recorded aversion for filling and returning census forms which verify their existence. This attitude in African-Americans may well be a carry-over of the runaway slave syndrome. For instance, in the central D'Ville area of St. Louis, a number of figures, including James Henry Thompson, Sr., organized blocks of residents to campaign throughout the community to destroy the census forms or avoid interviews in the 1940s, 1950s, and 1960s.

12. Jean Toomer, "Outline of an Autobiography," *The Wayward and the Seeking: A Collection of Writings by Jean Toomer*, 101-102.

13. Toomer, "Outline of an Autobiography," 123.

14. Turner, *The Wayward and the Seeking: A Collection of Writings by Jean Toomer*, 123.

15. Bernard Bell, "Portrait of the Artist as High Priest of Soul," *Black World*, XXIII, No. 2 (September 1974), 4-19, 92-97.

16. Richard Eldridge, "The Unifying Images in Part One of Jean Toomer's Cane," *College Language Association Journal*, XXII, No. 3 (March 1979), 212.

17. "The Blue Meridian" in *The Wayward and the Seeking: A Collection of Writings by Jean Toomer*, 225-226.

CHAPTER SIX

1. Jabulani Kamau Makalani, "Toward a Sociological Analysis of the Renaissance: Why Harlem," *Black World* (February 1976), 6.
2. Anonymous, *The Crisis*, 18, No. 2 (June 1919), 94-95.
3. Walter White, "The Success of the Negro Migration," *The Crisis*, 19, No. 3 (January 1920), 113.
4. Anonymous, "NAACP—Lynchings in the United States," *The Crisis*, 23, No. 4 (February 1922), 114.
5. John Henrik Clarke, "The Harlem Renaissance," *Black World* (November 1970), 123.
6. Marcus Garvey, et al., "Africa for Africans No Longer Invites Ridicule—Negroes Now Take Pride in the Desire to Return to Possess the Homeland," *The Negro World* (July 23, 1927), 1.
7. Alain Locke, "Negro Youth Speaks," in *The New Negro*, edited by Alain Locke (New York: Atheneum, 1925), 47-49.
8. Langston Hughes, "The Negro Artist and the Racial Mountain," *The Nation*, 122, No. 318, 692-694.
9. Jean-Paul Sartre, *Black Orpheus*, S. W. Allen, translator (Paris Presence Africaine, 1979), 40.
10. Martha Louise Climo, "L. S. Senghor's Imagery: An Expression of His Negritude," *Hommage a Leopold Sedar Senghor—homme de culture* (Paris: Presence Africaine, 1976), 342.
11. P. Chike Onwauchi, "Negritude in Perspective," *Black World* (October 1971), 4-14.
12. Onwauchi, "Negritude in Perspective," 6.
13. Mercer Cook, "Afro-Americans in Senghor's Poetry," *Hommage a Leopold Sedar Senghor—homme de culture* (Paris: Presence Africaine), 1976, 152-153.
14. William Leo Hansberry, *Africa and Africans as Seen by Classical Writers*, edited by Joseph E. Harris. (Washington, D.C.: Howard University Press, 1977).
15. Edward Braithwaite, "Race and the Divided Self," 55-56.
16. Jules Henry, *Culture against Man* (New York: Vintage Books 1983), 286.
17. Derrick Jensen, "Tricks of the Trade: Alfred McCoy on How the CIA Got Involved in Global Drug Trafficking," in *The Sun*, May 2003, Issue 329, 6.
18. Jean Toomer, "Why I Entered the Gurdjieff Work," in Robert B. Jones, ed., *Jean Toomer: Selected Essays and Literary Criticism* (The University of Tennessee Press: Knoxville, 1996), 109.
19. A. L. Pogossky, trans., *The Symbolism of the Tarot* by P. D. Ouspensky, St. Petersburg, Russia, 1913 reprint by Kessinger Publishing's Rare Mystical Reprints—United States, 6-7.
20. William Kulik, ed./trans., *The Selected Poems of Max Jacob* (Oberlin, Ohio: Oberlin College Press, 1999), 38.
21. William Kulik, ed./trans., *The Selected Poems of Max Jacob*, 15.
22. Langston Hughes. "Langston Hughes: Six Letters to Nicholas Guillen," trans. Carmen Alegria, *The Black Scholar,* July/August (1885), 56.
23. Lesley Feracho. "The Legacy of Negrismo/Negritude: Inter-American Dialogues" in *The Langston Hughes Review* 16, no. 1 and 2 (Fall/Spring 1999-2000), 2.

24. Vincent Fitzpatrick. "The American Mercury," in *Menckeniana: A Quarterly Review,* No. 123 (Fall 1992), 1. I would like to acknowledge my personal thanks to Mencken archival librarian Vincent Fitzpatrick for his invaluable help with this section of this study.
25. Charles Scruggs. *The Sage in Harlem: H. L. Mencken and the Black Writers of the 1920s* (Baltimore: The Johns Hopkins University Press, 1984), 163-164.
26. H. L. Mencken, "The Sahara of the Bozart," in *The New York Evening Mail,* November 13, 1917.
27. Charles Scruggs, *The Sage in Harlem,* 161.
28. Fenwick Anderson, "Black Perspective in Mencken's *Mercury,*" in *Menckeniana: A Quarterly Review,* No. 70 (Summer 1979), 2.
29. Maurice Merleau-Ponty, *The Primacy of Perception* (Evanston, Illinois: Northwestern University Press, 1964), 6.
30. Scott Cunningham. *Cunningham's Encyclopedia of Magical Herbs* (St. Paul: Llewellyn Publications, 1985), 237.

EPIPHANY

1. Bruno Lasker, "Doors Opened Southward," *The Survey* (November 1, 1923), 190-191.
2. Mark Helbling, "Sherwood Anderson and Jean Toomer," *Negro American Literature Forum,* 19, No. 2 (Summer 1975), 35-39.
3. Ibid. p. 37.
4. Robert Littell, "A Review of *Cane*" *The New Republic,* XXXVII (December 26, 1923), 126.
5. Victor A. Kramer, "The Mid-Kingdom of Crane's 'Black Tambourine' and Toomer's *Cane,*" *College Language Association Journal,* XVII, No. 4, June (1974), 486-497.
6. Clifford Mason, "Jean Toomer's Black Authenticity," *Black World,* 20 (November 1970), 73-74.
7. Houston Baker, *Singers of Daybreak,* (Washington, D.C.: Howard University Press, 1983), 54.
8. Jean Toomer, *The Wayward and the Seeking: A Collection of Writings by Jean Toomer,* edited by Darwin Turner (Washington, D.C.: Howard University Press, 1980), title page.

BIBLIOGRAPHY

WRITINGS ABOUT *CANE*

Abbott, Megan. "Doris Dance ... John Dreams: Free Indirect Discourse and Female Subjectivity in Cane." *Soundings: An Interdisciplinary Journal* 80.4 (Winter 1997): 455-474.

Ackley, Donald G. "Theme and Vision in Jean Toomer's *Cane*." *Studies in Black Literature* 1.1 (1970): 45-65.

Bakkar, Rudolf. "Kurt-Enrich Suckert of De Mondo *Cane* Van Malaparte." *Maatstaff* 27.7-9 (1979): 40-90.

Bell, Bernard W. "A Key to the Poems in *Cane*." *College Language Association Journal* 14:3 (1971): 251-258.

———. "Portrait of the Artist as High Priest of Soul: Jean Toomer's *Cane*." *Black World* 23.11 (1974): 4-19, 92-97.

Birat, Kathie. "Giving the Negro to Himself: Medium and 'Immediacy' in Jean Toomer's Cane." *Q-W-E-R-T-Y: Arts, Litteratures & Civilisations du Monde Anglophone* 7 (October 1997): 121-128.

Blackwell, Louise. "Jean Toomer's *Cane* and Biblical Myth." *College Language Association Journal* 17 (1974): 535-542.

Blake, Susan L. "The Spectatorial Artist and the Structure of *Cane*." *College Language Association Journal* 17 (1974): 516-534.

Bone, Robert A. "Jean Toomer's *Cane*." *The Negro Novel in America*. New York: Knopf, 1965. 81-88.

Bowen, Barbara E. "Untroubled Voice: Call and Response in *Cane*." *Black American Literature Forum* 16.1 (Spring 1982): 12-18.

Bradley, David. "Looking behind *Cane*." *The Southern Review* 21.3 (Summer 1985): 682-694.

Byrd, Rudolph P. "Shared Orientation and Narrative Acts in *Cane, Their Eyes Were Watching God*, and *Meridian*." *Melus* 17.4 (1991): 41.

Caldeira, Maria Isabel. "Jean Toomer's *Cane*: The Anxiety of the Modern Artist." *Callaloo* 8.3 (Fall 1985): 544-550.

Cancel, Rafael A. "Male and Female Interrelationship in Toomer's *Cane*." *Negro American Literature Forum* 5 (Spring 1971): 25-31.

Candela, Gregory Louis. "Melodramatic Form and Vision in Chesnutt's *The House behind the Cedars*, Dunbar's *The Sport of the Gods*, and Toomer's *Cane.*" *Dissertation Abstracts International* 42.11 (May 1982): 4826A.

Chase, Patricia. "The Women in *Cane.*" *College Language Association Journal* 14 (1971): 259-273.

Clark, J. Michael. "Frustrated Redemption: Jean Toomer's Women in *Cane*, Part One." *College Language Association Journal* 22.4 (1979): 319-334.

Clary, Francoise. "'The Waters of My Heart': Myth and Belonging in Jean Toomer's *Cane.*" *Jean Toomer and the Harlem Renaissance*, edited by Genevieve Fabre and Michel Feith. New Brunswick: Rutgers University Press, 2001. 68-83.

Collins, Paschal Jay. "Jean Toomer's *Cane:* A Symbolistic Study." *Dissertation Abstracts International*. Ann Arbor, Michigan, 1979. ISSN Pt. A 0419-4209; Pt. B 0419-4217.

Cooper, Kenneth J. (*St. Louis Post Dispatch* review). "Raising *Cane* unto the Stage." *Proud Magazine* 9.2 (1978): 29-31.

Coquet, Cecile. "Feeding the Soul with Words: Preaching and Dreaming in *Cane.*" *Jean Toomer and the Harlem Renaissance*, edited by Genevieve Fabre and Michel Feith. New Brunswick: Rutgers University Press, 2001. 84-95.

Dawson, Emma J. Waters. "Images of the Afro-American Female Character in Jean Toomer's *Cane*, Zora Neale Hurston's *Their Eyes Were Watching God*, and Alice Walker's *The Color Purple.*" *Dissertation Abstracts International* 48.10 (April 1988): 2627A.

Dorris, Ronald. "Early Criticism of Jean Toomer's *Cane:* 1923-1932." *Perspectives of Black Popular Culture*, edited by Harry B. Shaw. Bowling Green: Popular Culture, 1990. 65-70.

Dow, William. "Jean Toomer's *Cane* and Winesburg, Ohio: Literary Portraits from the Grotesque Storm Center." *Q-W-E-R-T-Y* 7 (1997): 129-136.

Duncan, Bowie. "Jean Toomer's *Cane:* A Modern Black Oracle." *College Language Association Journal* 15 (1972): 323-333.

Durham, Frank, ed. *Studies in Cane*. Columbus, Ohio: Charles E. Merrill-Merrill Studies Series, 1971.

Dyck, Reginald. "*Cane* and Its Discontents." *Eureka Studies in Teaching Short Fiction* 1.1 (2000): 57-73.

Eldridge, Richard. "Jean Toomer's *Cane:* The Search for American Roots." *Dissertation Abstracts International*. Ann Arbor, Michigan, 1978. ISSN Pt. A 0419-4209; Pt. B 0419-4217.

————. "The Unifying Images in Part One of Jean Toomer's *Cane.*" *College Language Association* 22.3 (1979): 187-214.

Fabre, Genevieve. "Dramatic and Musical Structures in 'Harvest Song' and 'Kabnis': Toomer's *Cane* and the Harlem Renaissance." *Jean Toomer and the Harlem Renaissance*, edited by Genevieve Fabre and Michel Feith. New Brunswick: Rutgers University Press, 2001. 109-127.

————. "Tight-Lipped 'Oracle': Around and Beyond *Cane.*" *Jean Toomer and the Harlem Renaissance*, edited by Genevieve Fabre and Michel Feith. New Brunswick: Rutgers University Press, 2001. 1-17.

Fabre, Michel. "The Reception of *Cane* in France." *Jean Toomer and the Harlem Renaissance*. New Brunswick: Rutgers University Press, 2001. 202-214.

Fahy, Thomas. "The Enslaving Power of Folksong in Jean Toomer's *Cane.*" *Literature and Music*, edited by Michael J. Meyer. Amsterdam: Rodopi, 2002. 47-63.

Fisher, Alice Poindexter. "The Influence of Ouspensky's *Tertium Organum* upon Jean Toomer's *Cane.*" *College Language Association Journal* 17.4 (1974): 504-515.

Foley, Barbara. "In the Land of Cotton: Economics of Violence in Jean Toomer's *Cane.*" *African American Review* 32.2 (Summer 1998): 181-198.

Ford, Nick Aaron. "Jean Toomer and His *Cane.*" *Langston Hughes Review* 2.1 (Spring 1983): 16-27.

Golding, Alan. "Jean Toomer's *Cane:* The Search for Identity through Form." *Arizona Quarterly* 39.3 (1983): 197-214.

Grandjeat, Charles-Yves. "The Poetics of Passing in Jean Toomer's *Cane.*" *Jean Toomer and the Harlem Renaissance,* edited by Genevieve Fabre and Michel Feith. New Brunswick: Rutgers University Press, 2001. 57-67.

Grant, Sister M. Kathryn. "Images of Celebration in *Cane.*" *Negro American Literature Forum* 5 (1971): 32-34, 36.

Gregory, Montgomery. Review of *Cane,* by Jean Toomer. *Opportunity* 1 (1923): 374-375.

Hajek, Friederike. "The Change of Literary Authority in the Harlem Renaissance: Jean Toomer's *Cane.*" *Literarische Diskurse und historischer Prozess: Beitrage zur englischen und amerikanischen Literatur und Geschichte,* edited by Bruhhild de la Motte. Potsdam: Pädagogische Hochschule "Karl Liebkneckt," 1988. 106-14.

Harmon, Charles. "*Cane,* Race and 'Neither/Norism.'" *Southern Literary Journal* 32.2 (2000): 90-101.

Howell, Elmo. "Jean Toomer's Hamlet: A Note on *Cane.*" *Interpretations: Studies in Language and Literature* 9 (1977): 70-73.

Hutchinson, George. "Identity in Motion: Placing *Cane.*" *Jean Toomer and the Harlem Renaissance,* edited by Genevieve Fabre and Michel Feith. New Brunswick: Rutgers University Press, 2001. 38-56.

Jackson, Blyden and Warren French. "Jean Toomer's *Cane:* An Issue of Genre." *The Twenties: Fiction, Poetry, Drama,* edited by Warren French. Deland: Everett/Edwards (1975): 317-333.

Kodat, Catherine. "To 'Flash White Light from Ebony': The Problem of Modernism in Jean Toomer's *Cane.*" *Twentieth Century Literature* 46.1 (Spring 2000). 1-19.

Kousaleos, Peter G. "A Study of the Language, Structure, and Symbolism in Jean Toomer's Cane and N. Scott Momaday's 'House Made of Dawn.'" *Dissertation Abstracts International.* Ann Arbor, Michigan, 1973. ISSN Pt. A 0419-4209; Pt. B 0419-4217; Pt. C 0307-6075.

Kraft, James. "Jean Toomer's *Cane.*" *Markham Review* 2.4 (1970): 61-63.

Kramer, Victor A. "The 'Mid Kingdom' of Crane's 'Black Tambourine' and Toomer's *Cane.*" *College Language Association Journal* 17.4 (1974): 486-497.

Krasny, Michael J. "The Aesthetic Structure of Jean Toomer's *Cane.*" *Negro American Literature Forum.* 9.2 (1975): 42-43.

Lieber, Todd. "Design and Movement in *Cane.*" *College Language Association Journal.* 13.1 (1969): 35-50.

Lindberg, Kathryne V. "Raising *Cane* on the Theoretical Plane: Jean Toomer's Racial Personae." *Cultural Difference and the Literary Text: Pluralism and the Limits of Authenticity in North American Literatures,* edited by Winifried Siemerling and Katrin Schwenk. Iowa City: University of Iowa Press, 1996. 49-74.

Littell, Robert. Review of *Cane. New Republic* 37 December 1923: 126.

McKay, Nellie Y. "Structure, Theme, and Imagery in *Cane.*" *Jean Toomer, Artist.* Chapel Hill: University of North Carolina Press, 1984.

McKeever, Benjamin F. "*Cane* as Blues." *Negro American Literature Forum* 4 (1970): 61-63.

Martin, Odette C. "*Cane:* Method and Myth." *Obsidian Black Literature in Review* 2 (1976): 5-20.

Matthews, George C. "Toomer's *Cane:* The Artist and His World." *College Language Association Journal* 17.4 (1974): 543-559.

Moore, Lewis D. "Kabnis and the Reality of Hope: Jean Toomer's *Cane.*" *North Dakota Quarterly* 54.2 (1986): 30-39.

Nwankwo, Nkem. "Cultural Primitivism and Related Ideas in Jean Toomer's *Cane.*" *Dissertation Abstracts International* 43.8 (February 1983): 2669 A.

Peckham, Joel B. "Jean Toomer's *Cane:* Self as Montage and the Drive toward Integration." *American Literature* 72.2 (2000): 275-290.

Reckley, Ralph, Sr. "The Vinculum Factor: 'Seventh Street'; and 'Rhobert' in Jean Toomer's *Cane.*" *College Language Association Journal* 31.4 (June 1988): 484-489.

Reilly, John M., Jr. "The Search for Black Redemption: Jean Toomer's *Cane.*" *Studies in the Novel* 2 (1970): 312-324.

Rice, Herbert W. "Repeated Images in Part One of *Cane.*" *Black American Literature Forum* 17.3 (1983): 100-105.

———. "An Incomplete Circle: Repeated Images in Part Two of *Cane.*" *College Language Association Journal* 29.4 (1986): 442-461.

Rusch, Frederick L. "Form, Function, and Creative Tension in *Cane:* Jean Toomer and the Need for the Avant-Garde." *Melus* 17.4 (1991): 15-28.

Saunders, James R. "Sonia Sanchez's Homegirls and Handgrenades: Recalling Toomer's *Cane.*" *Melus* 15.1 (1988): 73.

Scruggs, Charles W. "The Mark of Cain and the Redemption of Art: A Study in Theme and Structure of Jean Toomer's *Cane.*" *American Literature: A Journal of Literary History, Criticism, and Bibliography* 44 (1972): 276-291.

———. "Textuality and Vision in Jean Toomer's *Cane.*" *Journal of the Short Story in English* 10 (Spring 1988): 93-114.

Shaw, Brenda Joyce Robinson. "Jean Toomer's Life Search for Identity as Realized in *Cane.*" *Dissertation Abstracts International*. Ann Arbor, Michigan, 1976. ISSN Pt. A 0419-4209; Pt. B 0419-4217.

Shigley, Sally Bishop. "Recalcitrant, Revered, and Reviled: Women in Jean Toomer's Short Story Cycle, *Cane.*" *Short Story* 9.1 (2001): 88-98.

Solard, Alain. "Myth and Narrative Fiction in *Cane:* 'Blood-Burning Moon.'" *Callaloo* 8.3 (1985): 551-560.

Sollors, Werner. "Jean Toomer's *Cane:* Modernism and Race in Interwar America." *Jean Toomer and the Harlem Renaissance*, edited by Genevieve Fabre and Michel Feith. New Brunswick: Rutgers University Press, 2001. 18-37.

Spofford, William K. "The Unity of Part One of Jean Toomer's *Cane.*" *Markham Review* 2 (1972): 58-60.

Stein, Marian L. "The Poet-Observer and Fern Jean in Toomer's *Cane.*" *Markham Review* 2 (1970): 64-65.

Thompson, Chezia Brenda. "Hush, Hush—Somebody's Callin Ma Name: Analyzing and Teaching Jean Toomer's *Cane.*" *Dissertation Abstracts International* 46.5 (November 1985): 1282A.

Turner, Darwin T. "Jean Toomer's *Cane.*" *Negro Digest* 18.3 (1969): 54-61.

Van-Mol, Kay R. "Primitivism and Intellect in Toomer's *Cane* and McKay's *Banana Bottom:* The Need for an Integrated Black Consciousness." *Negro American Literature Forum* 20 (1976): 48–52.

Wagner-Martin, Linda. "Toomer's *Cane* as Narrative Sequence." *Modern American Short Story Sequences: Composite Fictions and Fictive Communities,* edited by Gerald J. Kennedy. Cambridge University Press, 1995. 19–34.

Wardi, Anissa Jaine. "The Mark of *Cane:* A Vernacular Study of Jean Toomer's African Pastoral in Narratives of Gloria Naylor, Ernest Gaines, and Toni Morrison." *Dissertations Abstracts International,* Section A 60.4 (October 1999):1138.

———. "The Scent of a Sugarcane: Recalling *Cane* in the Women of Brewster Place." *CLA Journal* 42.4 (June 1999): 483–507.

Watkins, Patricia. "Is There a Unifying Theme in *Cane?*" *College Language Association Journal* 15 (1972): 303–305.

Webb, Jeff. "Literature and Lynching: Identity in Jean Toomer's *Cane.*" *ELH* 67.1 (Spring 2000): 205–228.

Whyde, Janet M. "Meditating Forms: Narrating the Body in Jean Toomer's *Cane.*" *Southern Literary Journal* 26.1 (1993): 41.

WRITINGS RELATED TO *CANE* AND JEAN TOOMER

Anonymous. *Baltimore Afro-American,* August 27, 1932. A report of the death in child-birth of Margery Latmer Toomer, which refers to the article by Eugene Holmes in *Opportunity.*

Anonymous. *Baltimore Afro-American,* November 24, 1934. News item on Toomer's second marriage to Marjorie Content, which features him as a graduate of Dunbar High School.

Anonymous. Editorial. *New York Age,* November 24, 1934. Derides Toomer for reportedly stating that his ancestor P. B. S. Pinchback claimed to be a Negro only for political expediency.

Anonymous. *Baltimore Afro-American,* December 1, 1934. News report that Walter Pinchback, Toomer's uncle, is unsure about the race of P. B. S. but Pinchback considers himself to be "Colored." Also remarks on the migratory habits of his nephew Jean.

Anonymous. "Just Americans," *Time* 29.ii (March 28, 1932): 19.

Anonymous. "Americanization (of the Negro)." *Crisis* 27.4 (April 1919): 292.

Anonymous. "Colored Chicago." *Crisis* 10.5 (September 1951): 234–236.

Anonymous. "The (Negro's) Horizon—Music and Art." *Crisis* 16.1 (May 1918).

Anonymous. "African for the Africans No Longer Invites Ridicule—Negroes Now Take Pride in the Desire to Possess the Homeland." *Negro World* (July 23, 1927).

Anonymous. "Disenfranchisement in the District of Columbia." *Crisis* 10. 4 (August 1915): 89.

Anonymous. "Have You Ever Heard the Blues?" *Crisis* 11.1 (November 1915): 35.

Anonymous. "This Lynching Industry" 1920. *Crisis* 21.4 (February 1921): 160–168.

Anonymous. "Lynchings in the United States." *Crisis* 23.4 (February 1922): 165.

Anonymous. "(Negro) Peonage in Georgia." *Crisis* 21.1 (November 1920): 139.

Anonymous. "Some Contemporary Poets of the Negro Race" *Crisis* 17.4 (April 1919): 275–280.

Anonymous. "Our (Negro) Women and What They Think." *The Negro World* (July 17, 1926).

Anonymous. "The Test in Ohio." *Crisis* 37 (November 1930): 373-374.

Anonymous. "The Tenth Spingarn Medal." *Crisis* 30 (November 1930): 68-70.

Anonymous. "U.S. Department of (White) Justice." *Crisis* 42 (October 1935): 309-310.

Anonymous. "Chicago and Eight Reasons." *Crisis* 18 (October 1910): 293-297.

Anonymous. "The Negro and Religion." *Crisis* 17.5 (March 1919): 236-237.

Anonymous. "The Real Cause of Two Race Riots." *Crisis* 19.2 (December 1919): 56-57.

Anonymous. "The Shifting Black Belt." *Crisis* 18.2 (June 1919):94-95.

Anonymous. "Strata." *Survey* 56 (September 1, 1926): 595-596.

Anonymous. Review. *Boston Transcript* (December 15, 1923): 8.

Anonymous. Review. *Dial* 76 (January 1924): 92.

Anonymous. "Literary Vaudeville." *Springfield Republican* (December 23, 1923): 9.

WRITINGS ABOUT TOOMER

Aberger, Peter. "Leopold Senghor and the Issue of Reverse Racism." *Phylon* 41.3 (1980): 276-283.

"African for the Africans No Longer Invites Ridicule—Negroes Now Take Pride in the Desire to Possess the Homeland." *The Negro World* 23 July 1927.

"Americanization (of the Negro)." *Crisis* 27.4 (1919): 292.

Anderson, Jervis. *This Was Harlem*. New York: Farrar Straus Giroux, 1982.

Antoinides, Chris. "Jean Toomer: The Burden of Impotent Pain." *Dissertation Abstracts International*. Ann Arbor, Michigan, 1976. ISSN Pt. A 0319-4209; Pt. B 0419-4217.

Armstrong, John. "The Real Negro." *The New York Tribune* 14 October 1923: 26.

Baker, Houston A., Jr. "Introduction: Literary Theory Issue." *Negro American Literature Forum* 14.1 (1980): 3-4.

———. *Singers of Daybreak*. Washington, D.C.: Howard University Press, 1983.

Bakker, Rudolf. "Kurt-Enrich Suckert of De Mondo *Cane* Van Malaparte." *Maatstaff* 27 (vii-ix 1979): 40-90.

Baraka, Amiri. "Afro-American Literature and Class Struggle." *Black American Literature Forum* 14.1 (1980): 5-14.

Barthold, Bonnie J. *Black Time*. New Haven: Yale University Press, 1981.

Beard, Charles A. and Mary Beard. *The Rise of American Civilization* 2. New York: The Macmillan Company, 1927.

Bell, Bernard W. "Jean Toomer's 'Blue Meridian': The Poet as Prophet of a New Order of Man." *Black American Literature Forum* 14.1 (1980): 77-80.

Bell, Lisle. "Easy Going." *Nation* 123 (1926): 89.

Benson, Brian Joseph and Mabel Mayle Dillard. *Jean Toomer*. Boston: Twayne Publishers, 1980.

Bercovici, Konrad. "Almost Black and White." *Nation* 119 (1924): 386, 388.

Berry, Jason. "Jazz Literature." *Southern Exposure* 6.3 (1978): 40-49.

Black Literature Criticism. Detroit: Gale, Volume 3, 1992.

Blackwell, Henry. "An Interview with Ntozake Shange." *Black American Literature Forum* 13.1 (1979): 134-138.

Bluestein, Gene. "The Blues as a Literary Theme." *The Massachusetts Review* 8.4 (1967): 593-617.

Bone, Robert A. "The Black Classic That Discovered 'Soul' Is Rediscovered after 45 Years." *New York Times Book Review* 19 January 1969: 3.

————. *Down Home: A History of Afro-American Short Fiction from Its Beginnings to the End of the Harlem Renaissance*. New York: Capricorn Books–G. P. Putnam's Sons, 1975.

————. *The Negro Novel in America*. Revised edition 1958. New Haven: Yale University Press, 1965.

Bontemps, Arna. "The Harlem Renaissance." *Saturday Review* 30 (1947): 12–13, 44.

————, ed. *The Harlem Renaissance Remembered*. New York: Dodd, Mead & Company, 1972.

————. "The Negro Renaissance: Jean Toomer and the Harlem of the 1920s." *An Introduction to Black Literature in America from 1946 to the Present*. Cornwell Heights, PA: Publishers Agency, Inc., 1976. 126.

————. "The Negro Renaissance: Jean Toomer and the Harlem of the 1920s." *Anger and Beyond: The Negro Writer in the United States*, edited by Herbert Hill. New York: Harper, 1966. 20–36.

"Book Reviews." *Independent* 113 (1924): 202.

Boundry, Robert. *Jean-Joseph Relearivelo et La Mort*. Paris: Presence Africaine, 1971.

Bowles, Eva D. "Opportunities for the Educated Colored Woman." *Opportunity* 1.3 (1923): 8.

Braithwaite, William Stanley. "The Negro in American Literature." *The New Negro*, edited by Alain Locke. New York: Albert and Charles Boni, 1925. 19–41.

————. "The Negro in Literature." *Crisis* 38 (1924): 204–210.

————. "Some Contemporary Poets of the Negro Race." *Crisis* 17.4 (1919): 275.

Bricknell, Herschell. Review. *Literary Review of the New York Evening Post* (December 8, 1923): 333.

Brinkmeyer, Robert H., Jr. "Wasted Talent, Wasted Art: The Literary Career of Jean Toomer." *Southern Quarterly* 20.1 (1981): 75–84.

Brodwin, Stanley. "The Veil Transcended: Form and Meaning in W. E. B. Du Bois' *The Souls of Black Folk*." *Journal of Black Studies* 2.3 (1971): 303–321.

Brown, Sterling A. *Black Manhattan*. 1930. New York: Atheneum Publishers, 1969.

————. Interview 17 July 1974.

Burroughs, Nannie N. "Black Women and Reform." *Crisis* 10.4 (1915): 187.

Cadman, S. Parkens. "The American Negro and the World Wide Conflict of Color." *Opportunity* 1.1 (1923): 9.

Callahan, John F. "*In the Afro-American Grain: Reconsidering Sterling Brown*." *The New Republic* 3,544 (1982): 25.

————. *In the Afro-American Grain: The Pursuit of Voice in Twentieth Century Black Fiction*. Urbana: University of Illinois Press, 1988.

Calverton, V. F., ed. *Anthology of American Negro Literature*. New York: Modern Library, 1929.

Chesnutt, Charles Waddell. "Post-Bellum–Pre-Harlem." *Crisis* 38 (1931): 193–194.

"Chicago and Eight Reasons." *Crisis* 18 (1910): 293–297.

Christ, Jack M. "Jean Toomer's 'Bona and Paul': The Innocence and the Artifice of Words." *Negro American Literature Forum* 9 (1975): 44–46.

Christian, Barbara. "Spirit Bloom in Harlem. The Search of a Black Aesthetic during the Harlem Renaissance: The Poetry of Claude McKay, Countee Cullen and Jean Toomer." *Dissertation Abstracts International*. Ann Arbor, Michigan, 1973. DAIA-34101, p. 308.

Cleghorn, Sarah N. "Northerners Don't Understand the Negro." *Crisis* 19.5 (1920): 268.

Cohn, Jan. "Women as Superfluous Characters in America Realism and Nationalism." *Studies in American Fiction* 1.2 (1973): 154-162.

"Colored Chicago." *Crisis* 10.5 (1951): 234-236.

"The Colored Man's White." *Time* 14 April 1955: 18-19.

Cooke, Michael G. "The Descent into the Under World and the Modern Black Fiction." *The Iowa Review* 5 (1974): 72-90.

Cosgrove, William. "Modern Black Writers: The Divided Self." *Negro American Literature Forum* 17.4 (1973): 120-122.

Cyprian, Father. "Grassroots: Planning Negro American Literature Studies." *Black American Literature Forum* 2.2 (1968): 28-29.

Davenport, Franklin. "Mill House." *BANC!* 2 (1972): 6-7.

David, Arthur P. and Saunders Redding, eds. *Cavalcade*. Boston: Houghton Mifflin Company, 1971.

Davis, Angela. *Women, Race, and Class*. New York: Vintage Books, 1983.

Davis, Arthur P. "Growing Up in New Negro Renaissance." *Negro American Literature Forum* 2 (1968): 53-59.

Davis, Charles T. "Jean Toomer and the South: Region and Race as Elements within a Literary Imagination." *Studies in the Literary Imagination* 2 (1974): 23-27.

Davis, Vivian. "A Nigger Mess." *Black American Literature Forum* 5.3 (1971): 94-97.

Dawson, Emma Waters. "Eugene (Jean) Pinchback Toomer (1894-1967)." *African American Authors, 1745-1945: A Bio-Bibliographical Critical Sourcebook,* edited by Emmanuel S. Nelson. Westport, CT: Greenwood, 2000.

Dickerson, Mary Jane. "Sherwood Anderson and Jean Toomer: A Literary Relationship." *Studies in American Fiction* 1.2 (1973): 163-175.

Diggs, Irene. "The Biological and Cultural Impact of Blacks on the United States." *Phylon: The Atlanta University Journal of Race and Culture*. 41 (1980): 153.

Dillard, Mabel Mayle. *Jean Toomer: Herald of the Negro Renaissance*. Diss. Ohio University, 1967.

———. "Jean Toomer: The Veil Replaces." *College and Language Association Journal* 17 (1974): 468-473.

"Disenfranchisement in the District of Columbia." *Crisis* 10.4 (1915): 189.

Dorris, Ronald. "The Bacchae of Jean Toomer." *Dissertation Abstracts International*. Ann Arbor, Michigan, 1979. ISSN Pt. A 0419-4209; Pt. B 0419-4217.

Du Bois, W. E. B. "The Social Equality of Whites and Blacks." *Crisis* 21.121 (1920): 16.

———. *The Souls of Black Folk*. 1903. New York: Fawcett Publications, Inc., 1961.

———. "Opinion—Brothers, Come North." *Crisis* 19.3 (1920): 105.

Du Bois, W. E. B. and Alain Locke. "The Younger Literary Movement." *Crisis* 27 (1924): 161-163.

Durham, Frank. "Jean Toomer's Vision of the Southern Negro." *Southern Humanities Review* 6 (1972): 13-22.

———. "The Poetry Society of South Carolina's Turbulent Year: Self-Interest, Atheism, and Jean Toomer." *Southern Humanities Review* 5 (1971): 76-80.

Edwards, Ozzie L. "Skin Color as a Variable in Racial Attitudes of Black Urbanites." *Journal of Black Studies*. 3.4 (1973): 473-483.

Ellison, Curtis William. *Black Adam: The Adamic Assertion and the Afro-American Novelist*. Diss. University of Minnesota, 1970.

Ellison, Ralph. *Shadow and Act*. New York: The New York American Library, 1953.

Embree, Edwin. *Thirteen against the Odds*. New York: The Viking Press, 1944.

Esslinger, Pat Mano and Thomas A. Green. "Content Analysis in Black and White: A Research Note." *Negro American Literature Forum* 5.4 (1971): 123-125.

Fanon, Frantz. *Black Skin, White Masks*. New York: Grove Press, Inc., 1967.

————.*The Wretched of the Earth*. New York: Grove Press, Inc., 1963.

Fauset, Jessie. "New Literature on the Negro." *Crisis* 20.2 (1920): 78.

Firestone, Shulamith. *The Dialectic of Sex*. New York: Bantam Books, 1970.

Fitzgerald, John. "A Note on Marcus Garvey at Harvard, 1922: A Recollection of John M. Fitzgerald." *Journal of Negro History* 63.2 (1978): 157-160.

"Flight." *The Times Literary Supplement* 9 December 1926: 908.

Fokkema, D. W. and Elrud Kunne-Ibsch. *Theories of Literature in the Twentieth Century*. New York: St. Martin's Press, 1977.

Foley, Barbara. "'In the Land of Cotton': Economics and Violence in Jean Toomer's *Cane*." *African American Review* 32.2 (1998): 181-198.

Ford, Nick Aaron. "Jean Toomer and His *Cane*." *Langston Hughes Review* 2.1 (1983): 16-27.

Foster, Frances S. "Changing Concepts of Black Women." *Journal of Black Studies* 3.4 (1973): 433-454.

Frank, Waldo. Manuscript Letters in the Jean Toomer and the Gorham Munson Folders of the Waldo Frank Collection. Van Pelt Library, University of Pennsylvania, Philadelphia, PA.

————. *The Rediscovery of America*. New York, 1929.

Franklin, Clyde W. and Laurel R. Walum. "Toward a Paradigm of Substructural Relations: An Application to Sex and Race in the United States." *Phylon: Atlanta University Journal of Race and Culture* 33.3 (1972): 242.

Franklin, John Hope. *From Slavery to Freedom*, Third Ed. New York: Vintage Books, 1969.

Fullinwider, S. P. "Jean Toomer: Lost Generation, or Negro Renaissance?" *Phylon* 27 (1966): 396-403.

————. *The Mind and Mood of Black America*. Homewood, IL: Dorsey Press, 1969.

Garvey, Marcus. "The Burden of Leading the Negro." *Negro World* 16 August 1926.

————. "Marcus Garvey on Disarmanent Fiasco." *Negro World* 7 August 1926.

————. "Negroes, like Men of Other Races, Must Create New Environments and Opportunities for Themselves." *Negro World* 5 February 1927.

————. "When the Negro Came to Know Himself the Inferiority Illusion Vanished." *Negro World* 17 July 1926.

Gloster, Hugh M. *Negro Voices in American Fiction*. Chapel Hill: University of North Carolina Press, 1948.

Goede, William J. "Jean Toomer's Ralph Kabnis: Portrait of the Negro Artist as a Young Man." *Phylon: The Atlanta University Review of Race and Culture*. 30.1 (1969): 73-85.

————. *Tradition in the American Negro Novel*. Diss. University of California, Riverside, 1967.

Gornick, Vivian and Barbara K. Moran. *Woman in Sexist Society*. New York: New American Library, 1971.

Griaule, Marcel. *Conversations with Ogotemmeli*. London: Oxford University Press, 1975.

Griffin, John C. "A Chat with Marjery Content Toomer." *Pembroke Magazine* 5 (1974): 15-27.

————. "Jean Toomer: A Bibliography." *South Carolina Review* 7.2 (1975): 61-64.

————. "Jean Toomer: American Writer." (A biography.) *Dissertation Abstracts International.* Ann Arbor, Michigan, 1976. ISSN Pt. A 0419-4209; Pt. B 0419-4217.

Gruening, Ernest. "Going White." *Saturday Review of Literature* 10 July 1926: 918.

Gysin, Fritz. *The Grotesque in American Negro Fiction: Jean Toomer, Richard Wright, and Ralph Ellison.* Bern: Francke, 1975.

Hagopian, John V. "American Negro Novelists." *Studies in the Novel* 3.2 Special (1971): 190-215.

Hart, Robert C. "Black-White Literacy Relations in the Harlem Renaissance." *American Literature.* 44.4 (1973): 612-628.

"Have You Ever Heard the Blues." *Crisis* 11.1 (1915): 35.

Hayashi, Susanna Campbell. *Dark Odyssey: Descent into the Underworld in Black American Fiction.* Diss. Indiana University, 1971.

Helbling, Mark. "Jean Toomer and Waldo Frank: A Creative Friendship." *Phylon: The Atlanta University Review of Race and Culture* 41 (1980): 167-178.

————. *Primitivism and the Harlem Renaissance.* Diss. University of Minnesota, 1972.

————. "Sherwood Anderson and Jean Toomer." *Negro American Literature Forum* 9.2 (1975): 35-39.

High, Stanley. "Black Omens." *Saturday Evening Post* 4 June 1938: 15.

Holden, Emma B. "Notes." *New Republic* 48 (1926): 53.

Holmes, Eugene C. "Alain Locke and the New Negro Movement." *Black American Literature Forum* 2.3 (1968): 60-68.

————. "Jean Toomer, Apostle of Beauty." *Opportunity* 3 (1925): 252-254, 260.

Horne, Frank. "Correspondence." *Opportunity* 4 (October 1926): 326.

————. "Our Book Shelf." *Opportunity* 4 (July 1926): 326.

Huggins, Nathan I. *Harlem Renaissance.* New York: Oxford University Press, 1973.

Hughes, Langston. *The Big Sea.* New York: Hill & Wang, 1968.

————. "Harlem Literati in the Twenties." *Saturday Review* 22 June 1940: 13-14.

————. "The Negro Artist and the Racial Mountain." *Nation* 23 June 1926: 692-694.

Imes, Nelia. "Correspondence." *Opportunity* 4 (September 1926): 295.

Innes, Catherine L. "The Unity of Jean Toomer's *Cane.*" *College Language Association Journal* 15 (1972): 306-322.

"The Institute of the Black World: Martin Luther King, Jr. Memorial Center, Atlanta, Georgia: Statement of Purpose and Program (Fall 1969)." *Massachusetts Review: A Quarterly of Literature, the Arts and Public Affairs* 10 (1969): 713-717.

Jacobs, George S. "Negro Authors Must Eat." *The Nation* 12 June 1949: 710-711.

Jellinek, Roger. Review. *New York Times* 21 January 1969: 45.

Johnson, James Weldon. *Along This Way.* New York: The Viking Press, 1961.

Jones, Eugene Kinckle. "Building for a Larger Life—The Accomplishments of the Urban League in 1922." *Opportunity* 1.3 (1923): 19.

Jones, Robert B. *Jean Toomer: Selected Essays and Literary Criticsim.* Knoxville: University of Tennessee Press, 1996.

Josephson, Matthew. "Great American Novels." *Broom.* 5 (October 1923): 178-180.

The Journal of Southern Culture 28 (1975): 423-434.

Jung, Udo O. H. "Die Dichtung Jean Toomer und die Negerrenaissance." Festschrift article in AN 79-1-000152, (1979): 295-316.

"Just Americans." *Time* 28 Mar. 1932: 19.

Kerlin, Robert T. "Singers of New Songs." *Opportunity* 4 (May 1926): 162.

Kerman, Cynthia E. "Jean Toomer? Enigma." *Indiana Journal of American Studies* 7.1 (1977): 67-78.

———. *The Lives of Jean Toomer: A Hunger for Wholeness*, Baton Rouge: Louisiana State University Press, 1988.

Kopf, George. "Design in Jean Toomer's 'Balo.'" *Negro American Literature Forum* 7.3 (1973): 103-104.

———. "Jean Toomer and the Quest for Consciousness." *Dissertation Abstracts International*. Ann Arbor, Michigan, 1972. ISSN Pt. A 0419-4209; Pt. B 0419-4217; Pt. C 0307-6075.

———. "Jean Toomer's Life prior to Cane: A Brief Sketch of the Emergence of a Black Writer." *Negro American Literature Forum* 9 (1975): 40-41.

———. "The Tensions in Jean Toomer's 'Theater.'" *College Language Association Journal* 17.4 (1974): 498-503.

Kreymborg, Alfred. *Our Singing Strength: An Outline of American Poetry (1620-1930)*. New York: 1929.

Lasker, Bruno. "Doors Opened Southward." *The Survey* 1 November 1923: 190-191.

Levy, Eugene. *James Weldon Johnson: Black Leader, Black Voice*. Chicago: The University of Chicago Press, 1973.

"Literary Vaudeville." *Springfield Republican* 23 December 1923: 9.

Locke, Alain. *Four Negro Poets*. New York: Simon and Schuster, 1927.

———. "From *Native Son* to *Invisible Man*: A Review of the Literature for 1952." *Phylon: The Atlanta University Review of Race and Culture* 14 (1953): 34-44.

———. "Negro Youth Speaks." *The New Negro*, edited by Alain Locke. New York: Albert and Charles Boni, 1925, 47-53.

———. *The New Negro*. 1925. New York: Johnson Reprint Corporation, 1968.

Locke, Alain and W. E. B. Du Bois. "The Younger Literary Movement." *Crisis* 27 (1924): 161-164.

"The Lynching Industry." *Crisis* 21.4 (1921): 160-168.

"Lynchings in the United States." *Crisis* 23.4 (1922): 165.

Mason, Clifford. "Jean Toomer's Black Authenticity." *Black World* 20.1 (1970): 70-76.

McCarthy, Daniel P. "Just Americans—a Note on Jean Toomer's Marriage to Margery Latimer." *College Language Association Journal* 17 (1974): 474-479.

McDowell, Deborah E. "New Direction for Black Criticism." *Black American Literature Forum* 14.4 (1980): 153-159.

McKay, Claude. *A Long Way from Home*. 1937. New York: Harcourt, Brace & World, 1970.

McNeely, Darrell Wayne. "Jean Toomer's Cane and Sherwood Anderson's Winesburg, Ohio: A Black Reaction to the Literary Conventions of the Twenties." *Dissertation Abstracts International*. Ann Arbor, Michigan, 1975. ISSN Pt. A 0419-4209; Pt. B 0419-4217; Pt. C 0370-6075.

Michilin, Monica. "'Karintha': A Textural Analysis." *Jean Toomer and the Harlem Renaissance*, edited by Genevieve Fabre and Michel Feith. New Brunswick: Rutgers University Press, 2001. 96-108.

Miller, Herbert Adolphus. "The Myth of Superiority." *Opportunity* 1.8 (1923).

Miller, Ruth and Peter J. Katopes. "The Harlem Renaissance: Arna W. Bontemps, Countee Cullen, James Weldon Johnson, Claude McKay and Jean Toomer." Festschrift Article in AN 78-1-000142, (1942): 161-186.

Munro, C. Lynn. "Jean Toomer: A Bibliography of Secondary Sources." *Black American Literature Forum* 21.3 (1987): 275-287.

Munson, Gorham. "Correspondence." *New York Times* 16 February 1969: 54.

———. "The Significance of Jean Toomer." *Opportunity* 14 (1925): 262-263.

"The Negro and Religion." *Crisis* 17.5 (1919): 236-237.

"(Negro) Peonage in Georgia." *Crisis* 21.1 (1920): 139.

"The (Negro's) Horizon—Music and Art." *Crisis* 16.1 (1918).

O'Brien, Edward J. "The Best Short Stories of 1923." *Boston Evening Transcript* 1 December 1923.

O'Daniel, Therman B., ed. *Jean Toomer: A Critical Evaluation*. Washington, D.C.: Howard University Press, 1988.

Ogunyemi, Chikwenye Okonjo. "From a Goat Path in Africa: Roger Mais and Jean Toomer." *Obsidian: Black Literature in Review* 5.3 (1979): 7-21.

O'Neil, Wayne. "The Politics of Bidialectalism." *Negro American Literature Forum* 5.4 (1971): 127.

"Our (Negro) Women and What They Think." *The Negro World* 17 July 1926.

Parsons, Alice Beal. "Toomer and Frank." *The World Tomorrow* 7 (March 1924): 96.

Phillips, James T. "An Undervalued Function of Literature in Negro Secondary Schools." *The Colored American Magazine* 17.5 (1909).

Poetry Criticism. Detroit: Gale, Volume 7, 1994.

Prince, Vinton M., Jr. "Will Women Turn the Tide? Mississippi Women and the 1922 United States Senate Race." *Journal of Mississippi History* 42 (1980): 212-220.

Quirk, Tom and Robert E. Fleming. "Jean Toomer's Contribution to *The New Mexico Sentinel*." *College Language Association Journal* 19 (1976): 224-232.

Rand, Lizabeth A. "'I Am I': Jean Toomer's Vision beyond *Cane*." *College Language Association Journal*. 44.1 (2000): 43-64.

Rankin, William. "Ineffability in the Fiction of Jean Toomer and Katherine Mansfield." Festschrift Article in AN 76-1-000077, (1976): 160-171.

Rauville, Gamille de. "Jean-Joseph Rabearivelo—1901-1937, Ne et Mort a Tanarive." *Presence Franco—: Revue Litteraire* 12 (1976): 165-170.

"The Real Cause of Two Race Riots." *Crisis* 19.2 (1919): 56-57.

Redding, J. Saunders. "American Negro Literature." *The American Scholar* 18.2 (1949): 137-148.

Reilly, John, M., Jr. "Jean Toomer: An Annotated Checklist of Criticism." *Resources for American Literary Study* 4 (1974): 27-56.

———. "The Reconstruction of Genre as Entry into Conscious History." *Black American Literature Forum* 13.1 (1979): 3-6.

Review. *Boston Transcript* 15 December 1923: 8.

Review. *Dial* 76 (1924): 92.

Richardson, Willis. "The Hope of a Negro Dream." *Crisis* 19.1 (1919): 338.

Richmond, Merle. "Jean Toomer and Margery Latimer." *College Language Association Journal* 18 (1974): 480-485.

Riley, Roberta. "Search for Identity and Artistry." *College Language Association Journal* 17 (1974): 480-485.

Rosenfeld, Paul. "Jean Toomer." *Men Seen*. New York: Dial. 1925, 227-236.

Rusch, Frederick L. "The Blue Man: Jean Toomer's Solution to His Problems of Identity." *Obsidian* 6 (Spring-Summer 1980): 38-54.

———. "Every Atom Belonging to Me as Good Belongs to You: Jean Toomer and His Bringing Together of the Scattered Parts." *Dissertation Abstracts International*. Ann Arbor, Michigan, 1977. ISSN Pt. A 0419-4209; Pt. B 0419-4217.

———. "Meetings of Allen Tate and Jean Toomer." *American Notes and Queries* 17 (1978): 60.

———. "A Tale of the Country Round Jean Toomer's Legend, Monrovia." *Melus* 7.2 (1980): 37-46.

Sampson, J. Milton. "Race Consciousness and Race Relations." *Opportunity* 1.5 (1923): 15.

Schermerhorn, R. A. "A Note on the Comparative View of Caste." *Phylon: The Atlanta University Journal on Race and Culture* 33.3 (1972): 254.

Schultz, Elizabeth. "Jean Toomer's 'Box Seat.' The Possibility for Constructive Crises." *Black American Literature Forum* 13 (1979): 7-12.

Schuyler, George S. "The Negro-Art Hokum." *Nation* 16 June 1926: 662-663.

Scruggs, Charles W. "Alain Locke and Walter White: Their Struggle for Control of the Harlem Renaissance." *Black American Literature Forum* 14.3 (1980): 91-99.

———. "Jean Toomer's Fugitive." *American Literature: A Journal of Literary History, Criticism, and Bibliography*. 67.1: 84-96.

———. *Jean Toomer and the Terrors of American History*. Pennsylvania: University of Pennsylvania Press, 1998.

"The Shifting Black Belt." *Crisis* 18.2 (1919): 94-95.

Shockley, Ann Allen. "Dedicated to Jean Toomer." *BANC!* 2 (May/June 1972): i-ii.

Short Story Criticism. Detroit: Gale, Volume 1, 1988.

Solard, Alain. "The Impossible Unity: Jean Toomer's 'Kabnis.'" *Myth and Ideology in American Culture.*, edited by Regis Durand and Michel Fabre. University de Lille Ill, Villeneuve d'Ascq (1976): 175-194.

"Some Contemporary Poets of the Negro Race." *Crisis* 17.4 (1919): 275-280.

Stoodley, Bartelett, ed. *Society and Self*. New York: The Free Press of Glencoe, 1962.

"Strata." *Survey* 56 (1926): 595-596.

Szwed, John F. "Africa Lies Just off Georgia." *Africa Report* 15.7 (1970): 29-31.

Tate, Claudia C. "An Interview with Gayle Jones." *Black American Literature Forum* 13.1 (1979): 142-148.

Taylor, Carolyn G. "Blend Us with Thy Being: Jean Toomer's Mill House Poems." *Dissertation Abstracts International*. Ann Arbor, Michigan, 1977. ISSN Pt. A 0419-4217.

Taylor, Clyde. "The Second Coming of Jean Toomer." *Obsidian: Black Literature in Review* 1.3 (1975): 37-57.

"The Tenth Spingarn Medal." *Crisis* 37 (1930): 68-70.

"The Tests in Ohio." *Crisis* 37 (1930): 373-374.

Thomas, William Hannibal. *The American Negro: What He Was, What He Is and What He May Become*. New York: Negro Universities Press, 1901.

Thompson, Larry E. "Jean Toomer: As Modern Man." *The Harlem Renaissance Remembered,* edited by Arna Bontemps. New York: Dodd, Mead, 1972: 51-62.

———. "Jean Toomer: As Modern Man." *Renaissance* 2.11 (1971): 7-10.

Tischler, Nancy M. "The Negro in Modern Southern Fiction: Stereotype to Archetype." *Black American Literature Forum* 2.1 (1968): 3-6.

Toplin, Robert Brent. "Reinterpreting Comparative Race Relations: The United States and Brazil." *Journal of Black Studies* 2.2 (1971): 136-155.

Turner, Darwin T. *Afro-American Writers*. New York: Appleton-Century-Crofts, 1970.

———. "And Another Passing." *Negro American Literature Forum*. 1.1 (1967).

———. "The Failure of a Playwright." *College Language Association Journal* 10 (1966): 308-318.

———. *In a Minor Chord: Three Afro-American Writers and Their Search for Identity: Toomer, Cullen, Hurston*. Carbondale: Southern Illinois University Press, 1971.

————. "An Intersection of Paths: Correspondence between Jean Toomer and Sherwood Anderson." *College Language Association Journal* 17 (1974): 455-467.

————, ed. *The Wayward Seeking: A Collection of Writings by Jean Toomer*. Washington, D.C.: Howard University Press, 1980.

————. "W. E. B. Du Bois and the Theory of a Black Aesthetic." *Studies in the Literary Imagination* 7.2 (1974): 1-22.

Turpin, Waters E. "Four Short Fiction Writers of the Harlem Renaissance—Their Legacy of Achievement." *College Language Association Journal* 11 (1967): 59-72.

Twombly, Robert C. "A Disciple's Odyssey: Jean Toomer's Gurdjieffian Career." *Prospects: Annual of American Culture Studies* 2 (1976): 437-462.

"U.S. Department of (White) Justice." *Crisis* 42 (1935): 309-310.

Van Doren, Carl. "The Roving Critic." *Century Magazine* 111 (1926): 635-637.

Van Vechten, Carl. "Books." *New York Herald Tribune*. 11 April 1926: 3.

Wade, Melvin and Margaret. "The Black Aesthetic in the Black Novel." *Journal of Black Studies* 2.4 (1972): 391-408.

Waldron, Edward E. "The Search for Identity in Jean Toomer's 'Esther.'" *College Language Association Journal* 14 (1972): 277-280.

Welch, William. "The Gurdjieff Period." *BANC!* 2 (May/June 1972): 4-5.

Westerfield, Hargis. "Jean Toomer's 'Fern': A Mythical Dimension." *College Language Association Journal* 14 (1971): 274-276.

Weyl, Nathaniel. "New Mythology of the Negro Past." *National Review* 8 October 1968: 1020-1022.

White, Walter. "The Defeat of Arkansas Mob-Law." *Crisis* 21 (1923): 259-261.

————. "Election by Terror in Florida." *New Republic* 12 January 1921: 195-197.

————. *The Fire in Flint*. New York: Alfred A. Knopf, 1924.

————. *Flight*. New York: Alfred A. Knopf, 1926.

————. *How Far the Promised Land?* New York: The Viking Press, 1955.

————. *A Man Called White*. New York: The Viking Press, 1948.

————. "The Success of Negro Migration." *Crisis* 19.3 (1920): 112.

Withrow, Dolly. "Cutting through Shade." *College Language Association Journal* 21 (1977), 98-99.

Woodson, Jon. *To Make a New Race: Gurdjieff, Toomer, and the Harlem Renaissance*. Jackson: University Press of Mississippi, 1998.

WRITINGS BY TOOMER

Published Fiction, Poetry, and Drama

"Karintha." *Broom* IV (January, 1923): 83-85.

"Song of the Son." *The Crisis* 23 (April, 1922): 261; Survey 53 (March 1, 1925): 662.

"Banking Coal." *The Crisis* 24 (June, 1922): 65.

"Nora" ("Calling Jesus"). *Doubler Dealer* IV (September, 1922): 132.

"Storm Ending." *Doubler Dealer* IV (September, 1922): 118.

"Carma." *The Liberator* V (September, 1922): 5.

"Georgia Dusk." *The Liberator* V (September, 1922): 25.

"Fern." *Little Review* IX (Autumn, 1922): 25.

"Becky." *The Liberator* V (October, 1922): 26.

"Seventh St." *Broom* IV (December, 1922): 3.

"Harvest Song." *Doubler Dealer* IV (December, 1922): 258.

"Esther." *Modern Review* I (January, 1923): 50.

"Georgia Portraits." *Modern Review* I (January, 1923): 81.

"Blood-Burning Moon." *Prairie* (March–April), 1923): 18.

"Gum." *Chapbook* XXXVI (April, 1923): 22.

"Her Lips Are Copper Wire." *S4N* (May–August, 1923), n.p.

"November Cotton Flower." *The Nomad* (Summer, 1923), n.p.

"Kabnis."*Broom* V (August and September, 1923):12-16.

Cane. New York: Boni and Liveright, 1923. rpt. New York: University Place Press, 1967; New York: Harper and Row, 1969.

"Easter." *Little Review* XI (Spring, 1925): 3-7.

"Balo." *Plays of Negro Life*, Alain Locke and Gregory Montgomery. New York: Harper & Brother, 1927 269-286.

"Mr. Costyve Duditch." *Dial* 85 (December, 1928): 460-476.

"Winter on Earth." *Second American Caravan: A Yearbook of American Literature*. Edited by Alfred Kreymborg, Lewis Mumford, and Paul Rosenfeld. New York: Macaulay Co., 1929, 694-715.

"New York Beach." *The New American Caravan*. Edited by Alfred Kreymborg, Lewis Mumford, and Paul Rosenfeld, New York: Macaulay Co., 1929, 12-83.

"Reflection." *Dial* 86 (April, 1929): 314.

"White Arrow." *Dial* 86 (July 1929): 596.

Essentials: Definitions and Aphorisms. Privately printed by H. Dupee's Lakeside Press. Chicago: 1447 N. Dearborn Street, 1931.

"Brown River Smile." *Pagany* (Winter, 1932): 29-33.

"A Certain November." *Dubuque Dial* (November, 1935): 107-112.

"The Blue Meridian." *The New Caravan*. Edited by Alfred Kreymborg et al. New York: Macaulay Co., 1936, 107-133.

"See the Heart." *Friends Intelligencier* (August 9, 1947): 423.

"Five Vignettes," "The Lost Dancer, "At Sea," and excerpts from "The Blue Meridian." *Black American Literature: Poetry*. Edited by Darwin T. Turner. Columbus, OH: Charles Merrill, 1969, p. 58-59.

"The Blue Meridian."*Poetry of the Negro* 1746-1970. Edited by Langston Hughes and Arna Bontemps. Garden City, NY: Doubleday and Co., 1970, 107-133.

Nonfiction and Essays

"Race Problems and Modern Society." *Man and His World*. Edited by Baker Brownell. Northwestern University Essays in *Contemporary Thought*. VII. Chicago: Van Nostrand, 1928, 67-111.

"A New Force for Cooperation." *The Adelphi* (October, 1934): 25-31.

"The Hill." *America and Alfred Stieglitz: A Collective Portrait*. Edited by Waldo Frank, Lewis Mumford, and Paul Rosenfeld. Garden City, NY: Doran and Co., Inc., 1934, 294-303.

"Living Is Developing." *Psychologic Series* No. 1. Mill House Pamphlets, Doylestown, PA, 1936.

"Work Ideas 1." *Psychologic Series* No. 2. Mill House Pamphlets. Doylestown, PA, 1939.

Roads, People, and Principles. Mill House Pamphlets. Doylestown, PA, 1939.

"The Other Invasion." *Friends Intelligencier* (July 1, 1944): 423-424.
"The Presence of Love." *Friends Intelligencier* (November 25, 1944): 771-772.
"Today May We Do It." *Friends Intelligencier* (January 13, 1945): 19-20.
"Keep the Inward March." *Friends Intelligencier* (June 30, 1945): 411-412.
"The Uncommon Man." *Friends Intelligencier* (March 9, 1946): 147-148.
"Love and Worship." *Friends Intelligencier* (December 14, 1946): 695-696.
"Authority, Inner and Outer." *Friends Intelligencier* (July 5, 1947): 352-353.
"Chips." *Friends Intelligencier* (December 27, 1947): 705.
"The Flavor of Man." *William Penn Lectures*. Philadelphia: Young Friends Movement of
    the Philadelphia Yearly Meetings (1515 Cherry Street) 1949.
"The Flavor of Man" (excerpts). *Friends Intelligencier* (April 2, 1949): 183-184
"The Flavor of Man" (condensation). *Friends Intelligencier* (April 1949): 281-283.
"Something More." *Friends Intelligencier* (March 25, 1950): 164-165.
"Blessings and Curse." *Friends Intelligencier* (September 30, 1950): 567-577.
"Chapters from Earth-Being." *The Black Scholar* 2 (January 1971): 3-14.

Literary Criticisms

"An Open Letter to Gorham Munson." *S4N* (March-April 1923).
"Notations on The Captain's Doll." *Broom* V (August, 1923): 47-48.
(Untitled review of "Zona Gale's Faint Perfume"). *Broom* V (October, 1923):180-181.
"Waldo Frank's Holiday." *Dial* 75 (October, 1923): 383-386.
"The Critic of Waldo Frank." *S4N* (September-January 1923-24).
"Oxen Cart and Warfare." *Little Review* (Fall-Winter 1924-25): 44-48.

Dialogues

"Evil." Meditations. *The New Mexico Sentinel*, 1937.
"From a Farm." Meditations. *The New Mexico Sentinel*, 1937.
"Good and Bad Artists." Meditations. *The New Mexico Sentinel*, 1937.
"J.T. and P. B." Meditations. *The New Mexico Sentinel*, 1937.
"Make Good." Meditations. *The New Mexico Sentinel*, 1937.
"Socratic Dialogue." Meditations. *The New Mexico Sentinel*, 1941.

STUDIES IN AFRICAN AND AFRICAN-AMERICAN CULTURE

General Editor: James L. Hill

Studies in African and African-American Culture has the objective of presenting an outstanding series of original works which, in their critical appraisals and reappraisals of a wide variety of African/African-American topics, provide fresh and insightful analyses to broaden the contemporary point of view. With special emphasis on the basic traditions that are unique to African/African American cultures, the series seeks to present studies from disciplines as diverse as literature, history and sociology, and in this thematic variety, reveal the richness and global nature of the black experience. Each volume of the series will be a book-length study of a selected African/African-American topic, employing the most recent scholarship and methods of inquiry to explore the subject.

For additional information about this series or for the submission of manuscripts, please contact:

Peter Lang Publishing, Inc.
Acquisitions Department
29 Broadway, 18th floor
New York, New York 10006

To order other books in this series, please contact our Customer Service Department:

(800) 770-LANG (within the U.S.)
(212) 647-7706 (outside the U.S.)
(212) 647-7707 *fax*
CustomerService@plang.com

Or browse online by series:

www.peterlang.com